# sugar, sugar

# sugar, sugar

*every recipe has a story*

THE SUGAR MOMMAS®
KIMBERLY "MOMMA" REINER & JENNA SANZ-AGERO

PHOTOGRAPHY BY SARA REMINGTON

Andrews McMeel
Publishing, LLC
Kansas City · Sydney · London

Andrews McMeel Publishing, LLC
an Andrews McMeel Universal company
1130 Walnut Street, Kansas City, Missouri 64106

www.andrewsmcmeel.com

11 12 13 14 15 TEN 10 9 8 7 6 5 4 3 2 1

ISBN: 978-1-4494-0358-4

Library of Congress Control Number: 2011921501

For all photos except on pages 26, 100, 121, 132, 211, and 268:
Photography by Sara Remington
Photography assisted by Kass Medeiros and Shay Harrington
Food styling by Erin Quon
Food styling assisted by Alexa Hyman
Prop styling by Kami Bremyer

Design and art direction by Julie Barnes

www.sugarsugarrecipes.com

ATTENTION: SCHOOLS AND BUSINESSES
Andrews McMeel books are available at quantity discounts with bulk purchase for educational, business, or sales promotional use. For information, please e-mail the Andrews McMeel Publishing Special Sales Department: specialsales@amuniversal.com

I, Momma Reiner, wish to dedicate this book to the Reiner Boys: Daddy-O, Big Reiner, and Little Reiner. For some crazy reason my children believe I can do anything, and I choose to believe them. Thank you to the friends who kept me motivated and inspired me with their boundless creativity. I am grateful to my Momma for all the times we made fudge together, which eventually led to this book.

I, Momma Jenna, wish to dedicate this book to my grandmother and all her daughters, especially my Momma, who taught me to bake and how to love completely (and that somehow, sometimes, they are the same). I share that love in my own kitchen with my husband and son, who both manage to make me feel like a Rock Goddess and, even without sugar, make every day the sweetest I have ever lived.

# contents

## acknowledgments

*We, The Sugar Mommas, wish to thank our contributors, for opening their hearts and homes to us (that includes all the honorary "Sugar Mommas" in Jackson, Mississippi!), and the amazing women at www. ModernMom.com. We thank Cyndy Frederick-Ufkes, our professional recipe tester, and our "family and friends testers"—especially Alicia Dougherty, Joanne Piccolo, and Michele Steinlauf. We must not forget the carpool kids who tasted every recipe and crinkled their noses, spit things out, or declared "Mmmm" from the backseat. Thank you to the Los Angeles DWP boys who kept the water flowing, taste-tested countless cookies, and even submitted a recipe. Thanks also go to: Jane Dystel, for becoming the GPS on our sugar bus; Helen Levin, for providing a fresh set of eyes when ours were weary; Lane Butler, for polishing us up like jewels; Julie Barnes and the rest of the Andrews McMeel team; Lisa Wagner; and Matt Yates. To everyone else, thanks for supporting us or getting the hell out of our way.*

# introduction

*by Momma Reiner*

Every recipe has a story—a creator who brought it to life. My fudge came from a family recipe, passed down from generation to generation. The most important part of the fudge was the memory of making it. My mother recalls making fudge with her great-aunt. I enjoyed making fudge with my mother. I cherish the times my sons stood on chairs stirring the fudge pot and licking the spoons. I love the smell of "fudge soup": butter, sugar, and milk, softly boiling. I am always flattered when my friends start asking in early fall, "When is the fudge coming?"

After sprinkling my fudge around our seaside village for a few years, a neighbor asked if she could sell it in her gift shop. In a blink, Momma Reiner's Fudge became a cottage industry. I was completely unprepared when a call came and I heard the words, "You are being considered for the 'O List.'" Momma Reiner's Fudge skyrocketed when it appeared on the famed "O List" as one of Oprah's "Favorite Things" and, later, on the *Rachael Ray Show*. I even had the good fortune to swirl fudge and dip marshmallows alongside Martha on *The Martha Stewart Show*.

During that roller-coaster ride, I spoke to people across the country who told me about their favorite family recipes. It wasn't just the recipes I coveted; I wanted to hear people recount their sugar story. The seed was planted to write this book.

I started on this quest by word of mouth. First, I approached my book club. One gal said she ate a strawberry cake in Mississippi that was from an old recipe. So I rang that home baker up. While I was on the phone with the host, I learned about a pecan pie that was believed to have originated from a slave and been passed down two generations to a granddaughter named Lucinda Bell. My heart palpitated. Lucinda's pecan pie took me through history. The recipe had never been written down. I knew instantly that I had begun a journey to collect old sugar recipes and their stories before they faded away. What started as a sugar voyage turned into a documentary of American heritage.

Once the project began, I turned to my pal and law school classmate, Momma Jenna. After Jenna relayed her story to me of inheriting her grandmother's cookbook, we realized we shared a passion. So I said, "Hop on the sugar bus!" And she did, thank goodness. I have big, crazy ideas, and Momma Jenna has a really huge brain and a dose of common sense. She became kitchen co-captain, and together we became The Sugar Mommas. Since we are fellow sugar floozies in endless search of sugar contentment, it became clear that this book needed to be written together.

Why sweets? The family dessert is always legendary. No one wants to brag about Brussels sprouts! Sugar is like rocket fuel, projecting butter and flour into a different stratosphere. It takes you to a place where people get happy. They laugh, tell stories, stash leftovers in their purses, and guard their sacred sweets.

Why the stories? We could have just published sugar recipes, but we wanted to bring them to life. When we discovered Native American bourbon balls originally made with firewater, the recipe jumped off the page. When we heard about picking wild blueberries on Cape Cod, we could just picture the pie bubbling underneath a trickle of homemade vanilla ice cream. When we learned of a Mississippi woman eating her dessert while soaking in the bathtub, we perked up. The rituals and legacies behind the recipes we chose drew us in. These stories were vignettes providing glimpses into family lives, histories, and traditions. Above all, though, they were about the wonderful characters we stumbled upon along the way.

Momma Jenna and I want to introduce you to the people we met on our sugar journey, each with a recipe to share. In Texas, we found Philip Cannon, the former headmaster of a prestigious private school, who at first glance is Mr. Respectable but who actually is an intellectual chocolate wild man. We met Catherine Watson, a Mississippi sister who cracked us up with e-mails at midnight talking about bread pudding, why men love lemon desserts, and all the calories that have gone out her front door. We came across Greg Rogers, whose Kentucky Jam Cake was a symbol of love and acceptance to an uncle in San Francisco.

Our friend Helen gave us her family recipe box, and from there we discovered Aunt Bunny, one of the funniest human beings on earth, who named her dog Bhagwan Shree Rajneesh, after a controversial New Age guru. We chanced upon Irene Mangum, who is still trying to figure out how her cookies got the name Buffalo Chips when "all we got here is alligators and snakes." We acquired recipes from the Department of Water and Power workers, people we met at the vet, new friends we encountered walking through trade shows, and many people we have yet to hug in person.

The recession made this project more poignant. People returned to family life and reprioritized. Recipes that stood the test of time took on greater meaning. During this insightful period, we felt a connection with each person who shared his or her story. We lamented about the economy, but there was always laughter when we spoke about sugar. It was a mini mental vacation to recount Grandma's coconut cake so sky-high that it almost toppled over. Sugar memories from childhood instantly bring you to a time of joy. This book became so much more than a collection of recipes.

Whether you are an occasional home baker or an avid professional, we believe you will enjoy the delicacies collected here. Our hope is that if you have a cherished dessert, you'll be inspired to contribute it at www.SugarSugarRecipes.com so that we can collectively share a bit of our histories and rituals through sugar. These stories demonstrate that even the simplest treat makes a lasting impression. Every recipe has a beginning, a middle . . . and our goal is to make sure it does not have an end!

# The Sugar Mommas Legal Disclaimer
## (We Are Lawyers, You Know.)

**this book is creative nonfiction.** The Sugar Mommas obtained the recipes in this book from contributors. That was the easy part. We were equally interested in the narrative attached to each recipe. Countless times all we got was, "My family served this during the holidays." We knew better. Every recipe has a story.

**sometimes it felt like we were scratching the silver coating off a lottery ticket to reveal what was underneath.** It turned out that Dad hid the pies in his closet. Sisters confessed to throwing cake batter on the ceiling and leaving marks. One year the dog ate the Christmas cookies.

**sometimes the legacy was like a nut that, after a few taps, cracked wide open.** Cherry Slices were especially satisfying because they were made by a grandmother who parented a grandchild during a tumultuous time. A recipe arose from a family tragedy, made by a mother proven to be a pillar of strength.

**sometimes we went digging in the backyard.** To get to the treasure hidden in the dirt, we had to go beyond the source. We became investigative journalists. We called a contributor's mom, grandma, the cook, the nanny, cousins, nieces, and nephews. There can be many narrators in one story. As we inherently know, each person has his or her own revisionist history. Relatives from the same family have different perceptions and perspectives. Need we even mention the mother-daughter dynamic? They rarely see things eye to eye!

**sometimes we had to unlock the secret garden.** We spoke to many people well into their nineties, and we are not too sure ginkgo biloba will help at that point. When conversing with others in regions far from our own who had very thick accents, we did our best to decipher, interpret, and translate every word. Or the person who held the key had long ago passed away, and their relative made assumptions. In other cases, we were left with loose ends that we had to tie up with a pinch of puffery.

What we're trying to say is, we did our best to be as accurate as we could with the information we were given. And occasionally a contributor just didn't know where a relative got the recipe. It's a mystery left unsolved.

In conclusion, this book is about 98 percent nonfiction, with 2 percent creative glue to paste the stories together. If some unknown relative comes out of the woodwork with slightly conflicting memories than we have portrayed in this book, we say to you, please accept our apology. By all means, share your stories with us too. We invite you to join the recipe revolution and add your account on www.SugarSugarRecipes.com.

WITH SWEETEST REGARDS,

*The Sugar Mommas*

# sugar
# momma*isms*

*Momma Reiner*

I SPRAY EVERYTHING WITH
NONSTICK SPRAY.

I DON'T SIFT ANYTHING.

I ONLY USE BUTTER—NEVER
SHORTENING.

I PREFER FRENCH OR BELGIAN
CHOCOLATE.

I LIKE BIG, BOLD, OVER-THE-TOP
FLAVORS.

I PREFER FRUIT FLAVORS TO
CHOCOLATE.

I DECORATE MY PLATES WITH FRESH
FLOWERS.

I HAVE THREE CATS.

MY HUSBAND RARELY TRIES
ANYTHING SWEET THAT I MAKE.

I LIKE TO DANCE AROUND MY
KITCHEN WHEN I BAKE WHILE
BLASTING MUSIC.

MY BOYS THINK I AM CUCKOO.

I REFUSE TO USE A DOUBLE
BOILER.

I HATE NUTS.

I CELEBRATED MY FORTIETH
BIRTHDAY WRITING THIS BOOK.

I AM WEST COAST.

I AM A HOME BAKER.

{ *Momma Jenna on Momma Reiner: Bold,
tenacious, funny, and a bundle of energy—
Momma R doesn't just live life, she grabs it
by the britches every day and says, "Are you
coming along for the ride, or what?"*

> *Momma Reiner on Momma Jenna: A cross between Pink and Supreme Court Justice Sonia Sotomayor—a rock star with sheer brilliance (a mind like no other, legal and every other way), two talents that are not my strong suit.*

*Momma Jenna*

I BUTTER AND FLOUR MY PANS.

I RARELY SIFT.

I LIKE SHORTENING.

I USE BAKER'S CHOCOLATE.

I PREFER RICH, CREAMY, SMOOTH FLAVORS.

I DON'T LIKE BERRIES.

I LIKE MY WHIPPED CREAM SWEETENED.

I HAVE THREE CATS.

MY HUSBAND LOVES TO TRY EVERYTHING SWEET THAT I MAKE.

I SING ROCK MUSIC, BUT I LISTEN TO NINA SIMONE WHILE I COOK.

I DON'T OWN A CUISINART.

I REFUSE TO USE A DOUBLE BOILER.

I HATE RAISINS.

I CELEBRATED MY FORTIETH BIRTHDAY WRITING THIS BOOK.

I AM BICOASTAL.

I AM A HOME BAKER.

TOGETHER WE ARE ALMOST EXACT OPPOSITES,
YET MIRROR IMAGES—YIN AND YANG, SWEET AND SASSY.

CHAPTER

1

let's get real

# let's get real

Most of the recipes in this book date back at least two or three generations and, believe it or not, there have been some culinary advancements since then. We're not just talking about the Internet and air-conditioning. From nonstick pans to silicone utensils to the food processor, life is much easier in the kitchen these days. We are not sure what's in your kitchen drawer, or how you mix, melt, chop, or blend. Furthermore, we each do things a little differently. So we made some cooking decisions for consistency. In case you feel the need to understand the method to our baking madness, we've laid out some basic assumptions here.

## Equipment

Momma Reiner loves her food processor and pulses everything humanly possible. Momma Jenna likes the hands-on approach for some things (like Grandma Belles's pie crust) but can't live without her stand mixer for everything else. In fact, we both use stand mixers, usually fitted with the paddle attachment or the whisk attachment (see sidebar). If you don't have one, use a standard handheld electric mixer. And if your electricity goes out, that's OK. Most of these recipes were originally made by hand, and if you want to go all "pioneer woman" on us, you can do it by hand too. Of course, "by hand" means with a spoon or other utensil. You don't want to get all that goopy dough under your nails, do you?

## Techniques

**Sifting:** We don't do it. In days gone by, flour was denser and required sifting. We have confirmed through research that flour today is already presifted for the most part. We tested every recipe without sifting, even when the original recipe called for it. Frankly, we fear carpal tunnel from our PDAs and would prefer not to put the extra strain on our wrists and hands. We place the dry ingredients in a bowl and whisk them to fluff up, aerate, and blend well. If you really think the sifting gods will strike you down if you don't obey, then please, for the love of sugar, buy an electric sifter!

**Mixing:** The key to fluffy, moist baked goods is to avoid overmixing once you've combined the wet and dry ingredients. We think one of the main reasons your aunt Flo's cakes were better than any modern bakery is because people have a tendency to switch on the electric mixer and then walk away, while Flo probably did everything by hand with a wooden spoon. When combining moist and dry ingredients, they should be mixed just enough to incorporate the dry into the moist.

# what is a paddle *attachment*?

*In my quest to make the perfect chocolate chip cookie, I have been baking every recipe I can get my hands on. I even had a bake-off with myself on a rainy day when I made six dozen cookies: soft and chewy versus thin and crispy. The taste test is a subject for another discussion.*

*In the directions for all of the cookie recipes it says something to the effect of, "In the bowl of a stand mixer fitted with the paddle attachment. . . ." Well, what is a paddle attachment? My hand-me-down KitchenAid mixer (that I am very thankful for) came with only a whisk attachment. So I was using a handheld mixer, or when I thought my arm might fall off after six dozen cookies, I switched to the KitchenAid mixer with the whisk. I was sure that if I kept using the whisk for cookie dough, it would bend. So I broke down and decided to buy a new accessory.*

*After looking online for 40 minutes, I could not find a paddle attachment. Could this be? I called Christopher at 800-541-6390, the KitchenAid customer service hotline. After a chuckle, Christopher assured me that I was not crazy. The paddle is formally called a "flat beater." Thank you, Christopher!*

*I also learned some other helpful tidbits while on the phone with KitchenAid. The flat beater comes in two versions: with a nylon coating or in plain aluminum. The nylon coating makes the flat beater dishwasher safe. The aluminum flat beater should be washed by hand. (Please note that the whisk attachment is not aluminum. The tines or wires that make up the whisk are stainless steel. The whisk is, therefore, dishwasher safe.) Now that I have my coated flat beater, I can continue my quest to bake the perfect chocolate chip cookie.*

—MOMMA REINER

Overworking your batter will likely lead to a denser, flatter cake, so take it easy and just let your guests *think* you worked that hard.

**Melting:** We try to incorporate the microwave when we can, but occasionally a recipe calls for a double boiler. If you don't have one, or you don't have the energy to pry yours from the depths of a dusty cupboard, boil about an inch of water in a pot and then nestle a metal bowl in the pot over (but not touching) the water. The steam from the boiling water will heat the metal bowl and gently melt your chocolate or other ingredients. This technique prevents burning or scorching.

**Scraping:** Honestly, if stuff is sticking to the sides of your bowl when you're using a mixer, do we really need to remind you to stop and scrape down the sides and bottom of the bowl to make sure everything is incorporated properly? We didn't think so.

**Greasing (or buttering) and flouring pans:** Momma Reiner uses nonstick cooking spray (with or without flour, as applicable). Momma Jenna does it the old-fashioned way for posterity's sake. When a recipe says to grease a pan or butter and flour, feel free to use the appropriate spray version if that's your thing. The only exception is candy. When the directions say to butter the baking sheet (for example, Peanut Brittle), act accordingly or be prepared for a sticky mess. Don't worry—we noted all the exceptions so you won't use up brain cells trying to remember "butter only."

# Key Ingredients

**Flour:** Most recipes call for all-purpose flour, and we tend to use the commonly available bleached variety. If you're into unbleached flour, have at it. We're all for making adjustments that leave us more satisfied in the kitchen. When a recipe specifies cake flour, we felt it made a big enough difference to warrant including the proviso. That said, if you're having a midnight craving and simply don't have cake flour on hand, throw caution to the wind and dive in with the standard all-purpose variety. The extra "fluff" won't matter to those PMS gremlins living inside us.

**Butter:** Though we do not specify it throughout the book, The Sugar Mommas prefer unsalted butter. Many old-school people we spoke to tended to go with the salted version. This really is a matter of taste, and your decision will not affect the outcome to any critical degree. If your blood pressure rises from the sodium, don't blame us.

**Shortening:** While we're on the subject of shortening, Momma Reiner always substitutes with butter. You can too.

**Lard:** Yuck. If any recipe called for lard, we updated with shortening. There are those who say that nothing tastes better than a piecrust made with lard. Go for it—we won't hold you back. We figured vegetable shortening is readily available and is a modern derivation of animal fat.

**Milk:** When we say "milk," we mean whole milk. More on this up next.

# Lightening the Load

If you're looking to trim your waistline, you should probably set aside this book and step away from the butter. If you spend time at the gym, you may enjoy a few bites of everything in this book, but not all at the same time, please.

Seriously, if you wish to cut some calories, you may switch to lower-fat milk and other dairy products. As baking is a science, be aware that reducing the fat content may affect the outcome significantly. This is why we recommend whole milk in our desserts. If you must fit into that bikini and refuse to take along your beach cover-up (we never leave home without it), then we suggest you start by replacing only half of the milk called for with a lower-fat version (like 2 percent) and then slowly reduce the fat content and/or substitute more of the whole milk with lower-fat milk as you test the recipe each time to ensure that it still tastes delicious and works well. *Trial and error* is our mantra. Besides, what will be more popular at the end-of-summer pool party, the skinny bikini or the platter of congo bars?

# Law and Order

The Sugar Mommas went to law school, so we've been conditioned to prefer order in our lives. Many of our recipes were originally scribbled on butter-crusted index cards and read like this:

> "Ingredients: 1 c. flour, 4 T. water, ½ c. pecans.
>
> Directions: First put flour in a bowl and mix with water. Then add the pecans and scotch. Cook in a slow oven."

Huh? Where did *scotch* come from? How much? What the heck temperature is "slow" and does that mean you have to bake it all night? For obvious reasons, we have reinterpreted some of the instructions. We certainly meant no disrespect to our contributors and we are confident that they will understand (they may even thank us).

When we prepare our baked goods, we like to organize in advance. We have taken the liberty of deciding that dry ingredients should be combined first and then set aside for later inclusion. This way you're not fumbling about with your flour and baking soda while you've got creamed butter and sugar sitting idle in your mixer. It is also a nice way to double-check that you have enough of everything so that you can avoid dashing out to the local Stop 'n Go while raw egg sits on the counter. We've all been there.

## Sugar Mommas Tips

**sugar mommas note:** You will notice these scattered throughout the book. It's our way of sharing tips, tricks, and details culled from all of our contributors. If you're like us, you probably read the margins while anxiously waiting for your treats to bake. Don't be surprised if you come across something that you wish you'd known before you began. We suggest you skim the notes first, just in case you see something you may want to incorporate. Worst-case scenario, you will have to make it twice. But, hey, double dessert is a win-win.

**old school:** The way Grandma used to do it has worked for 80 years for a reason. Although we've updated most of these recipes, we occasionally felt inclined to include some tricks of the trade from generations past. By the same token, while we honor the original instructions as much as possible, we often like to suggest alternatives to bring a contemporary flair to the table.

**modern variation:** Once in a while we came upon a recipe that begged for a makeover. We like to provide simple options to present these desserts in a new light, whether by exposing the sides of the cake (*très risqué!*), making tartlets or bars instead of a whole pie, or baking cakes in squares rather than rounds. A few shakes of the magic wand bearing a striking resemblance to a wooden spoon, and poof: a swift upgrade from 8-track tape to MP3!

***carpool crunch:*** We are busy women. If we don't have enough time to bake, we often "create time" by finding shortcuts here and there to help get us from the mixing bowl to the dessert plate faster than you can say "parent-teacher conference." Look for our little cheats throughout the book.

***sass it up:*** We are attracted to sassy desserts that are visually tempting. Like adding pearls to the basic black dress, we splashed color here and there, sprinkled some crunch on top and in between, and tossed in a few sprigs of flora where we could for pizzazz. These suggestions scattered throughout the book include our favorite ingredients or tips to sass up the "wow" factor in these treats.

## Demonstrations

The Sugar Mommas learned to bake by following their moms around the kitchen. Sometimes the written word just can't convey what is really meant by "tuck under the edges tightly." Cooking dialects differ. A pinch to you may be more of a smidge to your neighbor. Photos of the finished product are helpful, and we have included many within these pages (and more on our Web site). We also created a virtual kitchen with video demonstrations of select recipes so that you can be coached along. If you have any trouble with something that we have not yet recorded, please feel free to write us, and we will do our best to include it. Join the sugar revolution and check out what we've posted at www.SugarSugarRecipes.com.

Our basic philosophy is this: Start baking, use whatever method you are comfortable with, ignore us when you must, and be mesmerized by the treats that magically appear within your kitchen. Happy baking!

CHAPTER

2

cakes to
diet for

There is no better way to say "You're special" than to present someone with a homemade cake. Sometimes it's a simple sheet cake or a coffee cake. Oftentimes cakes are tiered and regal. They look spectacular sitting on a pedestal, all gussied up and lavishly decorated. They make a statement for a birthday, anniversary, retirement, graduation, ballet recital, end-of-season football party, or any other celebratory occasion. Cakes are fancy! But, truth be told, cakes require no more work than a pie or frosted cookies. In fact, many of the cakes in this chapter are as easy as they are delicious.

When you start digging through people's recipe boxes, you find some magnificent delicacies that have been treasured by generations. Others have been forgotten, like a favorite winter coat collecting dust in the back of the closet, waiting for someone to rediscover them. We decided to restore some of these old recipes and freshen them up a bit.

We selected a Red Velvet Cake with the original boiled flour frosting, an Everything but the Hummingbird Cake that makes you want to take flight, and an Italian Love Cake so sweet that you may be inspired to break into a verse of "That's Amore." We also reveal a Banana-Caramel Cake that we really wanted to hoard for ourselves. That luscious cake is so divine, you may not want to share it either.

Flip through this chapter and read the wonderful stories behind the recipes. Stumble on an old memory or a new favorite, or just look at the pretty pictures and drool.

# Everything but the Hummingbird Cake

*Submitted by Irene Mangum*
*From her aunt Barbara Gayden's recipe, Baton Rouge, Louisiana*

Imagine Irene Mangum as a little girl on a plantation in early 1950s Louisiana, with pigtails and a fancy holiday dress, twirling underneath a weeping willow tree. Irene eagerly anticipated the arrival of Aunt Barbara, who would bring hummingbird cake on her visits from Texas. The family would congregate for these visits at Aunt Sis's house (her father's other sister) at the Fairview Plantation in East Feliciana Parish. Irene waited all year to bite into those moist banana pieces and all the nuts and other surprises inside. When she was growing up, Irene wondered why the pastry was called "hummingbird cake." By the time she was old enough to ask about the name, it was too late. Aunt Barbara had passed away, leaving behind the mystery.

Irene now serves this divine cake often. Everyone who has the good fortune to enjoy a slice inevitably asks how it got its name. Irene made up the story that "it has everything in it but the hummingbird!" As it turns out, hummingbird cake has deep roots in the South. The first noted publication was in the February 1978 issue of *Southern Living* magazine. Irene Mangum's version traces its origin back well over 80 years. Just the name piques your interest, doesn't it? When we asked Irene to share the recipe, she said, "Why, of course! I can't take it with me." Thanks, Irene!

> { *By the time she was old enough to ask about the name, it was too late. Aunt Barbara had passed away, leaving behind the mystery."*

# Everything but the Hummingbird Cake MAKES 1 (9-INCH) ROUND LAYER CAKE

3    cups cake flour (Irene uses Swans Down)

1    teaspoon baking soda

1    teaspoon salt

1    teaspoon ground cinnamon

2    cups granulated sugar

1½  cups vegetable oil

3    large eggs

1½  teaspoons vanilla extract

1    (8-ounce) can crushed pineapple, undrained

2    cups chopped pecans or walnuts, divided (second cup is optional)

2    cups (about 3 medium) sliced ripe bananas

1    batch Hummingbird Cream Cheese Frosting (recipe follows)

Fancy holiday dress

Preheat the oven to 350°F. Lightly grease and flour three 9-inch round cake pans and set aside.

In a medium bowl, combine the flour, baking soda, salt, and cinnamon. Set aside. Place the sugar and oil in the bowl of a stand mixer fitted with the paddle attachment. Mix on low speed for about 1 minute, until blended. Add the eggs, one at a time, and mix on low speed. Ensure that each egg is blended well before adding the next. Add the vanilla and blend. Add the flour mixture, one-half at a time, mixing on low speed until the dry ingredients are moistened. Add the pineapple, 1 cup of the nuts, and the bananas, and stir with a spatula (do not beat) until just combined. Spread the batter evenly into the pans. Bake until a toothpick inserted in the center comes out clean, 25 to 30 minutes. Cool the cakes in the pans on top of wire racks for 10 minutes, then carefully turn the cakes out onto the wire racks and let cool completely. While the cakes are cooling, make the frosting.

Place one cake layer upside down on a serving platter and spread frosting all around the top and sides. Be generous on top, as this will be a filling layer. Place the middle layer upside down on top of the frosted bottom layer and spread frosting over the top and sides of it, again, being generous with the top/filling layer. Place the third cake right side up on top of the second layer and complete the frosting of the top and sides. Sprinkle the remaining nuts over the frosting, if desired.

## Hummingbird Cream Cheese Frosting

| | |
|---|---|
| 2 | (8-ounce) packages cream cheese, at room temperature |
| 1 | cup (2 sticks) butter, at room temperature |
| 2 | (16-ounce) boxes confectioners' sugar |
| 2 | teaspoons vanilla extract |

In the bowl of a stand mixer fitted with the paddle attachment, combine the cream cheese and butter. Blend on medium speed until smooth. Turn the mixer to low speed and add the confectioners' sugar a little bit at a time until fully incorporated. Beat until light and fluffy. Stir in the vanilla.

*notes* _____

_____

_____

_____

_____

_____

_____

_____

# Kentucky Jam Cake

*Submitted by Greg Rogers*
*From his great-grandmother Mary Alice Claxon Smith's recipe, Claxon Ridge, Kentucky*

Claxon Ridge was mostly a tobacco farming community, so produce was not easy to come by back in the 1930s, when Essie Mae Smith Ellis started making her jam cake. There was one gentleman who supplied fruit and vegetables to the ridge, and the only time of year Essie Mae could buy raisins and pineapples was December. Thus, for the more than 50 years that she baked it, this cake was prepared only at Christmastime. The children were not allowed to eat this rare delicacy when it was first made. The cake was stored, covered with a cloth, taunting them for at least a week before the holiday. In the early years, it was baked in a wood-burning stove, which was also the only heat source for the home. The pantry where it was stored was so cold that it may as well have been a refrigerator. Essie Mae was very proud of her cake, and all the family members eagerly anticipated having it for Christmas dessert. Once the meal was over, Essie Mae whisked the cake away. She was quite stingy and didn't care to share any leftovers. Some relatives quietly admitted to sneaking out with pieces stashed in their purses.

Like many Southern women, Essie Mae showed her love through baking. When her son Jerry moved to San Francisco, she took great pleasure in sending him a jam cake in a tin every Christmas. She would include the recipe for the caramel icing so that he could finish the cake on-site with a presentation exactly as she would have wanted. Unfortunately, Jerry was among the first wave of gay men afflicted with AIDS, and he passed away in 1983. While sorting through Jerry's belongings, his sister Doris found the icing recipe in her mother's handwriting, along with a note that read, "Hope you have luck with this if you want to use it. I hope you can eat the cake. It is mussie. —Mama." Doris kept the note because the family knew how much it meant to Jerry that, no matter what, his mother accepted and loved him, never judging him.

Essie Mae's grandson, Greg, shared this story and recipe with us. He believes the recipe was handed down to Essie Mae from her mother, Mary Alice Claxon Smith, who lived in the small community of Claxon Ridge in Owen County, Kentucky. Essie Mae, in turn, passed the recipe along to her own children, including Greg's mother, Betty Jean Ellis Rogers.

When Greg moved to California, Betty continued the tradition of sending the cake at Christmastime. Greg's mother would make the whole cake, frost it, and then try every year to successfully mail it so that the frosting wouldn't stick to the lid. No such luck. When Greg received it, he would call Betty with the bad news that, once again, the frosting had done just that. It seems Essie Mae had the right idea of sending the icing recipe separately.

Betty now suffers from Alzheimer's and hardly recognizes her children. Every year when Greg visits for the holidays, his sister makes the jam cake and they take it to her. Greg would have loved for Betty to know that her mother's jam cake recipe was getting so much attention. In his words, "She would have thought this was really cool."

{ *She was quite stingy and didn't care to share any leftovers. Some relatives quietly admitted to sneaking out with pieces stashed in their purses.*

# Kentucky Jam Cake MAKES 1 (9-INCH) ROUND LAYER CAKE

1 cup raisins

1 (20-ounce) can crushed pineapple, undrained

2½ cups all-purpose flour

1 teaspoon baking soda

1 teaspoon ground cinnamon

1 teaspoon ground nutmeg

½ teaspoon ground allspice

½ cup vegetable shortening

½ cup (1 stick) butter, at room temperature

1 cup granulated sugar

5 large eggs

1 cup seedless blackberry jam

⅔ cup buttermilk

1 cup chopped pecans

1 warm batch Kentucky Caramel Icing (recipe follows)

Security cameras to catch cake snatchers

**Day 1:** In a small bowl, combine the raisins and pineapple (with juice). Cover and refrigerate overnight.

**Day 2:** Preheat the oven to 350°F. Butter and flour two 9-inch round cake pans (or use nonstick baking spray with flour) and set aside.

In a medium bowl, whisk together the flour, baking soda, cinnamon, nutmeg, and allspice. Set aside. In the bowl of a stand mixer fitted with the paddle attachment, beat the shortening and butter on medium speed until creamy. Add the sugar and continue to beat until light and fluffy. Add the eggs, one at a time, and mix until they are well blended. Mix in the jam. At this point it will look like blackberry soup. Turn off the mixer and add half of the dry ingredients. Mix on low speed until the dry ingredients are moistened. Add the buttermilk and blend. Add the second half of the dry ingredients, again mixing on low speed until just combined. Use a spatula to fold in the pineapple and raisin mixture. Fold in the pecans.

Pour the batter into the prepared pans and spread evenly. Bake for 50 to 60 minutes, until a toothpick inserted in the center comes out clean. Remove from the oven and cool the cakes in the pans on top of wire racks for 10 minutes, then carefully turn the cakes out onto the wire racks and let cool completely.

When the cakes have cooled, make the icing. Place the bottom cake layer on a serving platter. Use a knife or an angled spatula to ice the top with a very thick layer of icing, being generous, as this will be a filling layer. Do not ice the sides. Add the second layer of cake and frost the top only.

*notes*

*sass it up:* If you want to make this cake super-impressive (as if it weren't already), add fresh blackberries around the rim of the top layer of the cake before the frosting sets. This will carry your blackberry theme through with an exclamation point. Go "Southern hostess" and squirt some whipped cream topping onto each serving plate and then add mint leaves and a blackberry in the center, y'all!

*modern variation:* Use golden raisins in lieu of brown.

*old school:* This cake was originally made in a 9 by 13-inch baking dish. If you want to try it this way, bake for 55 to 60 minutes, until a toothpick inserted in the center comes out clean.

## Kentucky Caramel Icing

½ cup (1 stick) butter

1 cup packed light brown sugar

¼ cup whole milk

1 teaspoon vanilla extract

2 cups confectioners' sugar

Melt the butter in a medium saucepan over medium heat. Add the brown sugar and stir until dissolved. Bring to a boil and cook for 2 minutes, stirring constantly to prevent burning. Slowly add the milk and bring the mixture back to a boil. Remove the pan from the heat and let cool to lukewarm. Add the vanilla and stir to blend. Pour the caramel mixture into the bowl of a stand mixer fitted with the whisk attachment or leave in the pan and use a handheld electric mixer. Add the confectioners' sugar ½ cup at a time, beating on low speed for 1 to 2 minutes after each addition, until the sugar is completely dissolved and the icing has a smooth consistency.

## SUGAR MOMMAS TIPS

*sugar mommas note:* The icing cools and thickens quickly. You may want to frost one layer, then put the saucepan back on low heat and give it another whirl with the handheld electric mixer to soften it enough to apply the top layer of frosting. Or you can transfer the frosting to a glass or other micro-wave-safe bowl and microwave on high power in 25-second intervals, stirring in between, until it has a spreadable consistency.

*old school:* Double the frosting and spread icing on top and sides if you insist that every bite of cake needs to be slathered in caramel.

# bourn family *cakes*

*Submitted by Nancy Bourn*
*From her mother Evelyn Usry's recipes, Jackson, Mississippi*

Evelyn Usry had two weapons in her birthday cake arsenal. She blew everyone away with these for decades. The Red Velvet Cake was her specialty, and she dangled it like a carrot in front of her children. Her rule was if you had done your best up until the time of your birthday, you got Red Velvet Cake. If you did not live up to what her expectations were for you, little devils received the equally wonderful Devil's Food Cake. Growing up, Nancy and her siblings waited with anticipation to see which cake would be presented with flickering candles.

{
- **Red Velvet Cake**
- **Devil's Food Cake**

# Red Velvet Cake MAKES 1 (8-INCH) ROUND LAYER CAKE

Although this cake is currently in vogue, Red Velvet is a Southern classic. The modern trend suggests cream cheese frosting, but Ms. Evelyn would not have imagined spoiling her cake this way and only used cream cheese for cucumber sandwiches. The authentic recipe calls for a topping made with boiled milk and flour, which is known by many names: butter roux, boiled milk, cooked flour, and ermine. This frosting is so light and airy, you may think pixie fairies sprinkled magic sugar dust on a cloud and whisked it into frosting. It's truly a taste that we had never experienced until we tried it. Nancy Bourn bestowed her mother's recipe upon us, telling us the cake was "yummo!" We couldn't agree more.

| | | | |
|---|---|---|---|
| 2¼ | cups cake flour | 1 | cup buttermilk |
| ¾ | teaspoon salt | 1 | teaspoon baking soda |
| ½ | cup vegetable shortening | 1 | tablespoon white vinegar |
| 1½ | cups granulated sugar | 1 | tablespoon vanilla extract |
| 2 | large eggs | 1 | batch Classic Red Velvet Frosting (recipe follows) |
| 2 | tablespoons unsweetened cocoa powder | | Halo |
| ¼ | cup red food coloring | | |

Preheat the oven to 350°F. Lightly grease and flour three 8-inch round cake pans (or use nonstick baking spray with flour) and set aside.

In a small bowl, whisk together the flour and salt. Set aside. Place the shortening and sugar in the bowl of a stand mixer fitted with the paddle attachment. Beat on medium speed until creamy. Add the eggs, one at a time, beating to incorporate. Sift in the cocoa. (This is an exception to our strict "no sifting" policy, but you can just throw the cocoa in if you'd like.) Add the food coloring and blend well. Add half the flour mixture and blend on low speed until the dry ingredients are moistened. Slowly add the buttermilk. Add the remaining flour mixture and blend until just combined. Use a spatula to fold in the baking soda, vinegar, and vanilla.

Spread the batter evenly into the prepared pans. Bake until the cake springs back in the center when touched, 20 to 25 minutes. Remove from the oven and cool the cakes in the pans on top of wire racks for 10 minutes, then carefully turn the cakes out onto the wire racks and let cool completely.

Place one cake layer upside down on a serving platter and spread frosting over the top and sides. Be generous on top, as this will be a filling layer. Place the middle layer upside down on top of the bottom layer and spread frosting over the top and sides, again being generous with the top/filling layer. Place the third cake right side up on top of the second layer and complete the frosting of the top and sides.

## Classic Red Velvet Frosting

- 2    cups whole milk (see Old School tip)
- 6    tablespoons all-purpose flour
- 2    cups granulated sugar
- 2    cups (4 sticks) butter, at room temperature
- 2    teaspoons vanilla extract

Whisk the milk and flour together in a saucepan over medium heat, making sure to disperse any lumps. Continue cooking on medium heat, stirring constantly, until it forms a thick paste, about 6 minutes. Remove from the heat and cool completely (you may place the mixture in the refrigerator to speed the cooling process). In the bowl of a stand mixer fitted with the paddle attachment, beat the sugar and butter on medium speed for about 2 minutes. Add the vanilla. Reduce the speed to medium-low and add the flour mixture 1 tablespoon at a time. Beat until light and fluffy, about 3 minutes.

## SUGAR MOMMAS TIPS

*sass it up:* Add mini chocolate chips to the cake batter before baking so that there is a sensory surprise in each bite. We love surprises!

*old school:* Evelyn used half-and-half in her frosting instead of milk. If you choose to be ultra decadent, a 5K run charity event is a great way to burn off the excess calories.

*notes* _____

_____

_____

_____

_____

_____

_____

_____

_____

_____

_____

# Devil's Food Cake MAKES 1 (8-INCH) ROUND LAYER CAKE

Far from a punishment, this cake is a heck of a reward for being mischievous!

1 ½ cups cake flour

½ cup unsweetened cocoa powder (we use Valrhona)

1 (3.9-ounce) box instant chocolate pudding mix

1 ¼ teaspoons baking soda

⅔ cup vegetable oil

1 ¼ cups granulated sugar

2 large eggs

1 teaspoon vanilla extract

1 cup buttermilk

1 batch Devil's Food Frosting (recipe follows)

Pitchfork

Preheat the oven to 350°F. Lightly grease and flour two 8-inch round cake pans (or use nonstick baking spray with flour) and set aside.

In a small bowl, whisk together the flour, cocoa powder, chocolate pudding mix, and baking soda. Set aside. Place the vegetable oil and sugar in the bowl of a stand mixer fitted with the paddle attachment. Beat on medium speed for 1 minute, or until moist. Add the eggs, one at a time, beating until the mixture is creamy. Add the vanilla. Add half the flour mixture and blend on low speed until the dry ingredients are moistened. Slowly add the buttermilk. Add the remaining flour mixture and blend until just combined.

Spread the batter evenly into the prepared pans. Bake for 20 to 25 minutes, until a toothpick inserted in the center comes out clean. Remove from the oven and cool the cakes in the pans on top of wire racks for 10 minutes, then carefully turn the cakes out onto the wire racks and let cool completely. While the cakes are cooling, make the frosting.

Place one cake layer upside down on a serving platter and spread frosting over the top and sides, being generous on top, as this will be a filling layer. Place the second cake right side up on top of the bottom layer and complete the frosting of the top and sides.

## Devil's Food Frosting

¾ cup (1½ sticks) butter, at room temperature

2 cups confectioners' sugar

⅓ cup unsweetened cocoa powder (Nancy uses Hershey's)

¼ cup heavy whipping cream (or more as needed)

1 teaspoon vanilla extract

Place the butter and confectioners' sugar in the bowl of a stand mixer fitted with the paddle attachment and blend until smooth. Turn the mixer to low speed and add the unsweetened cocoa powder a little bit at a time until fully incorporated. Slowly add the cream, starting with the ¼ cup and blending well. If necessary, add more cream 1 tablespoon at a time until the frosting is of the desired consistency for spreading. Stir in the vanilla.

# Banana-Caramel Cake

*Submitted by Joanna Ennis*
*From her great-aunt Fern Taylor's recipe, Jeanette's Creek, Ontario, Canada*

Joanna Ennis was married in 1993 at the age of 25. Her mother, Helen, threw Joanna a wedding shower and invited colleagues (other labor and delivery nurses) and all of Joanna's aunties. As an intended surprise, Helen sent blank cards to all the attendees before the shower. The idea was to present Joanna with a compilation of recipes. Of course, some things do not go according to the plan, and the cookbook was never completed.

In 2005, Helen sent Joanna a birthday present. Helen copied all of the recipes from the bridal shower cards by hand. She also included many old family recipes that had been abandoned. One such entry was this delicious cake. Joanna asked her mother why she'd never served it to the family. "Were you keeping it for yourself?" she joked. Helen explained that she tended to limit her baking to treats the whole family would enjoy. Since Joanna's father and sister didn't like bananas, Joanna was deprived of this dessert for most of her childhood.

Helen enjoyed this treat while growing up because her aunt Fern made the cake regularly. Helen remembers as a child jumping on bikes with her two siblings and hightailing it across the railroad tracks to their aunt's house in the hope of getting lucky with a fresh slice. "Often we were," Helen wrote. "Years later [Aunt Fern] told us she would make two [cakes] because by the time we finished the pieces she gave us, there wasn't enough left for her dessert. Neat aunt, eh!"

This cake represents a combination of our favorite things: banana (Momma Jenna) and caramel (Momma Reiner). We call it a Sugar Mommas spectacular combustion! Perfect for PMS or that 3:00 P.M. blood sugar boost.

{ *Joanna asked her mother why she'd never served it to the family. "Were you keeping it for yourself?"*

# Banana-Caramel Cake MAKES 1 (8-INCH) ROUND LAYER CAKE

| | |
|---|---|
| 2 large ripe bananas, mashed | 1 large egg |
| 1 teaspoon baking soda | 1 teaspoon vanilla extract |
| 1⅓ cups all-purpose flour | ½ cup whole milk |
| 1 teaspoon baking powder | 1 warm batch Aunt Fern's Caramel Icing (recipe follows) |
| 1 cup granulated sugar | Recipe cards |
| ¼ cup (½ stick) butter, melted | |

Preheat the oven to 350°F. Butter two 8-inch round cake pans (or use nonstick spray) and set aside.

Place the bananas and baking soda in a small bowl and mix them together and set aside. In a medium bowl, whisk together the flour and baking powder. Set aside.

In the bowl of a stand mixer fitted with the paddle attachment, beat the sugar and butter on medium speed until combined. Add the egg and vanilla and blend on low speed until creamy. Add half of the flour mixture and blend until the dry ingredients are moistened. Blend in the milk. Add the remaining dry ingredients and mix on low speed until just combined. Use a spatula to fold in the bananas.

Pour the batter evenly into the prepared pans. Bake for 25 to 30 minutes, until a toothpick inserted in the center comes out clean. Remove from the oven and cool the cakes in the pans on top of wire racks for 10 minutes, then carefully turn the cakes out onto the wire racks and let cool completely.

When the cakes have cooled, make Aunt Fern's Caramel Icing. Place one cake layer upside down on a serving platter. Use a knife or an angled spatula to spread the warm icing onto the cake, being generous on top, as it will be a filling layer. Place the second layer upside down on top of the bottom layer and spread icing on the top and sides.

notes

*sugar mommas note:* This recipe is very versatile. Joanna has made cupcakes, sheet cake, rounds, and squares. We love the idea of a square layer cake for a unique visual effect. The layers will be a little thinner, so make sure to watch your bake times, as they may vary when using a different pan than specified. See our Cake Pan Volume Chart (page 274) for guidance.

*sass it up:* If you want to make a "wow" presentation and impress your friends, don't frost the sides of the cake. Instead, frost the top of the bottom layer with a very thick layer of icing. Slice 1 or 2 bananas (depending on your level of banana love) and place the slices around the edges of the cake or all across the top. Add the second layer of cake and ice the top completely.

*carpool crunch:* When pressed for time, this is a great one-bowl cake. Just throw everything together, mix it up, and pour it into your pan(s).

## Aunt Fern's Caramel Icing

½ cup (1 stick) butter

1 cup packed light brown sugar

¼ cup whole milk

½ teaspoon vanilla extract

1½ cups confectioners' sugar

Melt the butter in a medium saucepan over medium heat. Add the brown sugar and stir until dissolved. Bring to a boil and cook for 2 minutes, stirring constantly to prevent burning. Slowly add the milk and bring the mixture back to a boil. Remove the pan from the heat and let cool to lukewarm temperature. Add the vanilla and stir to blend. Pour the caramel mixture into the bowl of a stand mixer fitted with the whisk attachment. Add the confectioners' sugar ½ cup at a time, beating on low speed for 1 to 2 minutes after each addition, until the sugar is completely dissolved and the icing has a smooth consistency.

## SUGAR MOMMAS TIPS

*sugar mommas note:* The icing cools and thickens quickly. You may want to frost one layer, then put the saucepan back over low heat and give it another whirl with a handheld electric mixer to soften it enough to apply the top layer of frosting. Or you can transfer the frosting to a glass or other microwave-safe bowl and microwave on high power in 25-second intervals, stirring in between, until it has a spreadable consistency.

*sugar mommas dirty little secret:* If there is any leftover caramel after frosting the cake, Joanna dabs a spoonful between two graham crackers and shoves it in her mouth. (Don't let the kids see!) That's our kind of chick! We say, who needs the graham crackers? A spoon or finger works well as long as the caramel has cooled. If you make yourself sick and/or nauseous from intravenous caramel infusion and still have icing left over, refrigerate it in a tightly sealed container. Then you can pop it in the microwave and pour it over ice cream when you regain consciousness.

# mary lou's celebration *cakes*

*Submitted by Carolyn Hollis*
*From her mother Mary Lou Bruno's recipes, Jackson, Mississippi*

Carolyn Hollis told us that when she thinks of her mother, Mary Lou, she always thinks of *I Love Lucy*. Mary Lou was a big fan of the show, and Carolyn said her mom could "cut up like Lucy." Mary Lou's priority was her family, and cooking was how she expressed her TLC. As you can imagine, birthdays are a big deal in the South. Mary Lou always gave her three children a choice of which flavor cake she would conjure up for their birthdays: chocolate, strawberry, or caramel.

Carolyn carried on the cake tradition with her three children. The custom expanded to include holidays and other celebrations. It would be difficult to choose just one cake, so we made sure to acquire all three recipes.

{
- Chocolate Celebration Cake
- Caramel Celebration Cake
- Strawberry Celebration Cake

# Chocolate Celebration Cake MAKES 1 (9 BY 13-INCH) SHEET CAKE

This cake is a chocoholic's dream! Also referred to as the A-Team Cake, it was consumed by Carolyn's son before every football game. Maybe the caffeine made him run faster? The fudge topping soaks into the cake to make a dense frosting. It's not for the faint of heart.

| | | | | |
|---|---|---|---|---|
| 2 | cups all-purpose flour | | ½ | cup (1 stick) butter |
| 2 | cups granulated sugar | | ½ | cup vegetable or canola oil (Carolyn uses Wesson Best Blend, which is half canola and half vegetable) |
| ½ | teaspoon salt | | | |
| 1 | teaspoon baking soda | | 3 | tablespoons unsweetened cocoa powder |
| 2 | large eggs | | | |
| ½ | cup buttermilk | | 1 | warm batch Chocolate Celebration Icing (recipe follows) |
| 1 | teaspoon vanilla extract | | | |
| 1 | cup water | | | Team jersey |

Preheat the oven to 350°F. Grease and flour a 9 by 13-inch baking dish (or use nonstick baking spray with flour) and set aside.

Place the flour, sugar, salt, and baking soda in the bowl of a stand mixer fitted with the paddle attachment and set aside. In a separate, large bowl, whisk the eggs, buttermilk, and vanilla. Set aside. In a saucepan over medium heat, combine the water, butter, oil, and cocoa powder. Bring the mixture to a boil, stirring constantly. Remove the pan from the heat and slowly pour this liquid over the flour mixture. Blend on low speed. Slowly add the egg mixture and mix until just combined. Pour the batter into the prepared pan and bake for 25 to 30 minutes, until a toothpick inserted in the center comes out clean.

While the cake is baking, make the icing so that it will be ready to pour over the hot cake. Remove the cake from the oven and use a fork or a bamboo skewer to poke holes in the cake to allow the icing to drip down. Gently pour the warm icing over the cake. Let cool completely. The icing will harden slightly.

# Chocolate Celebration Icing

1   (16-ounce) box confectioners'
    sugar

3   tablespoons unsweetened cocoa
    powder

½   cup (1 stick) butter

6   tablespoons buttermilk

1   teaspoon vanilla extract

1   cup chopped pecans (optional)

In a small bowl, whisk together the sugar and cocoa powder. Set aside. Melt the butter in a saucepan over medium heat. Add the sugar-cocoa mixture, buttermilk, and vanilla and whisk together to remove any clumps. Bring to a boil, stirring constantly. Decrease the heat to low and stir until smooth (a handheld electric mixer works well for this purpose). If desired, fold in the nuts.

# Caramel Celebration Cake MAKES 1 (9 BY 13-INCH) SHEET CAKE

It's no secret that Momma Reiner has a soft spot for caramel. In this case, we both agree—and there's no polite way to say it—this cake is #$*!ing fantastic!

| | |
|---|---|
| 1 | (18.25-ounce) box Duncan Hines Butter Recipe Golden Cake Mix |
| 1 | cup sour cream |
| ½ | cup granulated sugar |
| ¾ | cup vegetable or canola oil (Carolyn uses Wesson Best Blend, which is half canola and half vegetable) |

4 large eggs

1 warm batch Caramel Celebration Icing (recipe follows)

*The Help* by Kathryn Stockett

Preheat the oven to 350°F. Grease and flour a 9 by 13-inch baking dish (or use nonstick baking spray with flour) and set aside.

In the bowl of a stand mixer fitted with the paddle attachment, combine the cake mix, sour cream, sugar, and oil. Beat on low speed until the dry ingredients are moistened. Add the eggs one at a time. Beat on medium speed until just combined.

Pour the batter into the prepared pan. Bake for 30 minutes, or until a toothpick inserted in the center comes out clean. Transfer the cake to a wire rack and let cool completely.

Use a fork or a bamboo skewer to poke holes in the cake to allow the icing to drip down. While the cake is cooling, make your icing. Pour the warm icing over the cooled cake.

*sass it up:* Use Heath toffee bits in your cake. Pour half the cake batter into the pan. Sprinkle some candy bits over the top. Pour the remaining batter over them and bake as directed. You could also sprinkle some crumbled Heath bars on top of the icing for a little bonus.

*carpool crunch:* For the icing, use 7 ounces of Kraft Premium Caramel Bits—they are already unwrapped so you don't have to bother.

## Caramel Celebration Icing

Note: You will need a candy thermometer for the Caramel Celebration Icing recipe.

| | |
|---|---|
| ½ | cup (1 stick) butter |
| 2 | cups granulated sugar |
| ⅔ | cup whole milk |
| ⅛ | teaspoon salt |
| 30 | soft caramel candies |

In a saucepan over medium heat, combine the butter, sugar, milk, and salt. Stir frequently until a candy thermometer reaches 234°F. Remove the pan from the heat. Add the caramels and stir until melted. This will take a few minutes, so just keep stirring. A handheld electric mixer works well for this purpose. Do not put the icing back on the heat!

*notes*

## Strawberry Celebration Frosting

| | |
|---|---|
| 2 | tablespoons fresh or frozen strawberries, slightly smashed |
| ½ | cup (1 stick) butter, at room temperature |
| 1 | (8-ounce) package cream cheese, at room temperature |
| 1 | (16-ounce) box confectioners' sugar |

Place the strawberries on a paper towel to remove excess liquid. In the bowl of a stand mixer fitted with the paddle attachment, combine the butter and cream cheese, and blend. Add the sugar and continue to blend until creamy. The frosting may be a little stiff. Blend in the strawberries (start with 1 tablespoon and then add the rest to your liking).

*notes*

_____

_____

_____

_____

_____

_____

_____

*modern variation:* Go to your local farmers' market and use fresh strawberries in place of frozen. Clean and rinse about 12 average-size strawberries, place them in a bowl, and sprinkle about 1 tablespoon of sugar over them. Let them sit for 15 to 20 minutes, then mix them into the batter.

*sass it up:* Slice thin layers of fresh strawberries and place them on top. This cake is also beautiful when decorated with fresh garden flowers. If your flowers are not edible, be sure to remove them prior to serving.

# Italian Love Cake

*Submitted by Jason Layden*
*From Joanne Layden's recipe, Northtown, Pennsylvania*

Like a scene out of *Steel Magnolias*, if it were set in the Northeast, hairdresser Joanne chitchats with her customers at the local beauty parlor as they get coiffed. Beyond the typical gossip, the women enjoy discussing their culinary prowess. It is in the salon that Joanne has found a treasure trove of desserts among the pins and curlers.

One such recipe was Italian Love Cake. The ricotta cheese piqued Joanne's interest and inspired her to try it for her daughter's sixteenth birthday. She liked it so much that she even encouraged her father, the toughest critic in the family, to try a slice. After tasting the cake, Joanne's father slipped her a ten-dollar bill. "What's this for?" she asked. To her surprise, he replied, "To make another cake." It's been 25 years and Joanne is still making Italian Love Cake for her daughter's birthday.

This is a voluptuous cake. The creamy chocolate frosting tastes like a thick malted milk shake. Like revenge, we think it's a dish best served cold.

{ *It is in the salon that Joanne has found a treasure trove of desserts among the pins and curlers.*

# Italian Love Cake MAKES 1 (9 BY 13-INCH) SHEET CAKE

1   (18.25-ounce) box marble cake mix (prepared to the batter stage according to the box instructions; see Sugar Mommas Notes)

2   pounds ricotta cheese

3   large eggs

¾   cup granulated sugar

2   teaspoons vanilla extract

1   batch Italian Love Chocolate Frosting (recipe follows)

Gondola

Preheat the oven to 400°F. Butter and flour a 9 by 13-inch baking dish (or use nonstick baking spray with flour). Pour the prepared cake batter into the pan and spread it evenly. Set aside.

In a large bowl, mix the ricotta cheese with the eggs, sugar, and vanilla. Pour the ricotta mixture evenly over the top of the cake batter. Bake for 45 to 55 minutes, until a toothpick inserted in the center comes out clean. Remove from the oven and cool completely in the refrigerator. Once the cake is cooled, use a knife or an angled spatula to spread the Italian Love Chocolate Frosting over the top.

*sugar mommas note:* A Duncan Hines Moist Deluxe Fudge Marble Cake Mix box calls for 1¼ cups water, ⅓ cup vegetable oil, and 3 large eggs.

*sugar mommas disappearing act:* Don't be alarmed if you think the ricotta went missing. Its weight transports it to the bottom of the baking dish while the cake rises.

## Italian Love Chocolate Frosting

1   (3.9-ounce) box instant chocolate pudding mix

1   cup whole milk

1   (8-ounce) container whipped topping, cold but not frozen (Joanne uses Cool Whip)

In the bowl of a stand mixer fitted with the whisk attachment, whip the instant chocolate pudding mix and milk on low speed for 1 to 2 minutes, until smooth with no lumps. Add the whipped topping and continue to beat for about 2 minutes, until smooth.

*notes* _____

_____

_____

_____

_____

_____

_____

_____

# Scrumdilliumptious White Chocolate Cake

*Submitted by Shawn Jones*
*From Ruth Hutchison's recipe, Obion, Tennessee,*
*or Bunny Hampton's recipe, Sweetwater, Texas*

Like many family treasures, this heirloom recipe comes with a dispute over origin and ownership. It's not clear whether it belonged to Shawn's aunt Bunny or her great-grandmother Ruth "Mom" Hutchison. Everyone in the family has a different recollection. In this case, you just throw up your hands and say, "Unsolved mystery, but it tastes darn good!"

Shawn has fond memories of visiting Aunt Bunny in Sweetwater, Texas. "No one could tell a story better than Bunny." This recipe always reminds Shawn of Aunt Bunny's hilarious tales of her twin brothers (one of which is Shawn's dad) playing cowboys and Indians, and mistaking her closet for the bathroom in the middle of the night, or of how her rescue dog got the fancy name of guru Bhagwan Shree Rajneesh. The controversial New Age mystic and spiritual leader was known for a large collection of vehicles and other worldly possessions. Nicknames were not tolerated, as Bunny believed abbreviating her dog's name was sacrilegious. Bunny said she loved her dog, Bhagwan Shree Rajneesh, so much that when she passed away she was leaving everything she owned to the dog.

No matter where the cake derived from, it is chic, beautiful, and tasty, and would be lovely for any occasion, from a hillside picnic in Napa Valley to a wedding at the Plaza Hotel in New York City.

> { *Bunny said she loved her dog, Bhagwan Shree Rajneesh, so much that when she passed away she was leaving everything she owned to the dog.*

# Scrumdilliumptious
# White Chocolate Cake MAKES 1 (9-INCH) ROUND LAYER CAKE

½ cup water

1⅓ cups white chocolate chips

½ cup water

4 large eggs, separated

2½ cups cake flour (see Sugar Mommas Note)

1 teaspoon baking powder

1 cup (2 sticks) butter, at room temperature

2 cups granulated sugar

1 cup buttermilk

1 teaspoon vanilla extract

1 cup unsweetened flaked coconut (optional)

1 cup chopped pecans or almonds (optional)

1 batch of Scrumdilliumptious White Fudge Glaze (recipe follows)

Diamond-studded dog collar

Preheat the oven to 350°F. Butter and flour three 9-inch round cake pans (or use nonstick baking spray with flour) and set aside.

In a saucepan over medium heat, bring the water to a boil. Decrease the heat to low, add the white chocolate chips, and stir constantly until completely melted. Remove the pan from the heat and set aside to cool.

Place the egg whites in a medium bowl. Using a handheld electric mixer, beat the egg whites on high speed until stiff peaks form, about 4 minutes. Set aside. In a separate medium bowl, whisk together the flour and baking powder and set aside.

Place the butter and sugar in the bowl of a stand mixer fitted with the paddle attachment and beat on medium speed until light and fluffy. Add the eggs yolks, one at a time, mixing until each is incorporated. Add the melted chocolate and mix on low speed until blended. Add half of the flour mixture and mix on low speed until the dry ingredients are moistened. Add the buttermilk. Add the remaining flour mixture and blend until just combined. Add the vanilla. Use a spatula to gently fold in the stiff egg whites. Stir in the coconut and/or chopped nuts, if desired.

Pour the batter evenly into the prepared pans. Bake for 35 to 40 minutes, until a toothpick inserted in the center comes out clean. Remove from the oven and cool the cakes in the pans on top of wire racks for 10 minutes, then carefully turn the cakes out onto the wire racks and let cool completely.

Place one cooled cake layer upside down on a serving platter and pour about one-quarter of the glaze over the top, spreading evenly with a knife or an angled spatula. Place the middle layer upside down on top of the bottom layer and spread another one-quarter of the glaze over it. Place the third cake layer right side up on top of the second layer and complete the glazing of the top and sides.

*notes* _____

_____

_____

_____

_____

_____

_____

## SUGAR MOMMAS TIPS

*sugar mommas note:* You may use all-purpose flour, but we recommend Swans Down cake flour.

*sass it up:* We like to fancy up our cakes and make them look extravagant. Leave the sides bare and insert big, plump fresh raspberries or halved strawberries in between the layers on top of the frosting. Then add a ring of berries on the top edge of the frosted cake. This makes for a very impressive presentation.

## Scrumdilliumptious White Fudge Glaze

- ¾ cup (1½ sticks) butter, at room temperature
- 3 cups granulated sugar
- ¾ cup whole milk
- ¼ teaspoon salt
- 2 teaspoons vanilla extract

Place the butter, sugar, milk, and salt in a saucepan over medium heat and bring to a rolling boil. Boil for 4 minutes, stirring constantly. Remove the pan from the heat and stir in the vanilla. Let cool without stirring. When the mixture is cool, beat until it is thick enough to spread (a handheld electric mixer on medium speed works well for this purpose).

*notes*

# Shoo-Fly Cake

*Submitted by Joanne Layden*
*From her friend Jean Pellechio's recipe, Norristown, Pennsylvania*

Joanne's mother frequently made shoofly pie, a regional specialty. Joanne would never eat the pie because she believed it was made out of flies. "Who would eat flies?" she wondered. She was actually afraid of it and thought it looked like a slimy mess. Then, 20 years ago, a co-worker brought in a cake for someone's birthday. After having a piece of it, the by-then-adult Joanne asked her friend what type of cake it was. When Jean said, "Shoofly Cake," Joanne's jaw dropped. Imagine her surprise! She couldn't believe how good it was. The very next day Joanne made it for her family, and everyone agreed—flies taste good.

{ *"Who would eat flies?" she wondered.*

# Shoo-Fly Cake MAKES 1 (9 BY 13-INCH) SHEET CAKE

| | | | |
|---|---|---|---|
| 4 | cups all-purpose flour | 2 | cups water |
| 1 | (16-ounce) box light brown sugar | 1 | cup dark corn syrup (we use Karo) |
| ½ | teaspoon salt | 2 | teaspoons baking soda |
| 1 | cup (2 sticks) butter | | Fly swatter |

Preheat the oven to 400°F. Butter and flour a 9 by 13-inch baking dish (or use nonstick baking spray with flour) and set aside.

In a large bowl, mix together the flour, brown sugar, and salt. Do not use a food processor; use a pastry cutter or fork to cut in the butter. Use a fork or your hands to mix the ingredients until crumbly. Reserve 1½ cups of the mixture in a separate, smaller bowl.

In a saucepan over medium heat, bring the water to a boil. Add the corn syrup and baking soda and mix until combined. Gently pour the liquid mixture into the larger bowl of sugar mixture. Mix well. This will make a very thin liquid batter. Pour into the prepared baking dish. Sprinkle the reserved sugar mixture over the batter. Bake for 35 to 45 minutes, until a toothpick inserted in the center comes out clean and the center no longer jiggles. Cool completely in the baking dish on top of a cooling rack before serving.

*notes*

# Mama Kite's Cheesecake

*Submitted by Cyndy Hudgins*
*From her mother Anne Kite's recipe, Lone Mountain, Tennessee*

We've come across a lot of interesting nicknames in our travels, and we often wonder where they come from. In Mama Kite's case, when her first grandchild was born, the paternal grandmother's name ("Grandmother"—go figure) was already established. She wanted the children to be able to differentiate her husband and her from the other grandparents, so they became Mama and Papa Kite.

The cheesecake was one of Mama Kite's staple desserts, especially for company, since it could be made ahead of time and the presentation made it look noteworthy. Cyndy told us that when she first started making this recipe, she was not as patient as her mother had been, and Cyndy's version was somewhat lumpy. She praised the advent of the food processor, which made this recipe much easier to duplicate.

This is a tried-and-true cheesecake. We love it because it's not too sweet. We compare it to our favorite pair of boyfriend jeans—simple, dependable, and rock solid.

{ *We compare it to our favorite pair of boyfriend jeans—simple, dependable, and rock solid.*

# Mama Kite's Cheesecake MAKES 1 (9-INCH) CAKE

## GRAHAM CRACKER CRUST

1  heaping cup graham cracker crumbs (see Old School tip)

¼  cup granulated sugar

1  teaspoon ground cinnamon

¼  cup (½ stick) butter, melted

## FILLING

12  ounces cream cheese, at room temperature

⅓  cup granulated sugar

3  large eggs

1½ teaspoons vanilla extract

Kite

Butter and flour a 9-inch springform pan and set aside (see Sugar Mommas Note).

**To make the crust:** Place the crumbs, sugar, and cinnamon in the bowl of a food processor and pulse for 5 to 10 seconds to combine. With the processor running and the lid on, slowly add the butter through the feed tube until a coarse meal forms. Use a fork or your fingers to press the crumb mixture down firmly on the bottom and up the sides of the pan to form the crust. Chill in the refrigerator for at least 1 hour before filling.

**To make the filling:** In the bowl of a stand mixer fitted with the paddle attachment, beat the cream cheese on medium speed until it is soft and fluffy. Add the sugar and mix until incorporated. Add the eggs, one at a time, mixing on low speed until each is blended. Add the vanilla and blend. Pour the filling into the prepared crust and spread evenly. Place the cheesecake in a cold oven and turn it to 275°F. Bake for about 45 minutes, until firm. Remove from the oven and let cool completely on a wire rack.

⸭ notes ⸭ _____

_____

_____

_____

_____

_____

_____

_____

_____

_____

_____

_____

_____

_____

_____

_____

_____

## SUGAR MOMMAS TIPS

*sugar mommas note:* If you don't have a springform pan, don't fret. You can use a 9-inch pie plate and adjust your cooking time, baking for 35 to 45 minutes, until the filling is firm.

*old school:* If you don't own a food processor, use this as an excuse to vent some pent-up aggression without appearing unladylike. Place the graham crackers inside a large resealable plastic bag, seal it tightly, and crush the crackers with a rolling pin or the flat side of a meat mallet. Pour the crumbs into a mixing bowl and stir in the sugar and cinnamon. Stir the melted butter into the crumbs, mixing well.

Or get a little more zen: Nabisco and Keebler make prepackaged graham cracker crumbs, or you could use a ready-made graham cracker crust, should you choose to refrain from the hatchet job.

*modern variation:* Use fresh fruit, such as raspberries, and an updated sauce to top your cheesecake and/or decorate the plate. You may want to offer the sauce on the side. Try our Cardinal Sauce (recipe follows).

# Cardinal Sauce

*Submitted by Momma Reiner*

*From her stepmother Suzanne Halff Robinson's recipe, Savannah, Georgia*

What I remember most about my childhood (on the weekends), was begging my stepmother, Suzanne, to make Cardinal Sauce for my vanilla ice cream. I would stand beside her, waiting impatiently for the sauce to finish pulsing in the Cuisinart. I watched with anticipation—a dribble of lemon juice, a pinch more sugar, a few drops of Grand Marnier—is it done yet? I'd run to the freezer, get out the Frusen Glädjé vanilla ice cream, and scoop it into a bowl. When pulsed to perfection, the blazing red sauce blanketed the white ice cream and pooled into the bowl. I begged for enough sauce to shroud each bite of cream. My weekend treat was intense. (A confession: I snuck into the kitchen and drank any leftover sauce I found in the fridge—shhhh.)

{ *I watched with anticipation— a dribble of lemon juice, a pinch more sugar, a few drops of Grand Marnier— is it done yet?*

# Cardinal Sauce
**MAKES ABOUT 2 CUPS**

12   ounces raspberries, fresh or
     thawed frozen

½   cup granulated sugar
     (or more as needed)

2    tablespoons Grand Marnier

1    teaspoon fresh lemon juice
     (or more as needed)

In the bowl of a food processor, combine the fruit, sugar, Grand Marnier, and lemon juice. Pulse until the fruit is pureed and the ingredients are blended. Taste the sauce and add more lemon and/or sugar depending on the natural sweetness of the fruit. This sauce is always a crowd-pleaser.

*notes*

*modern variation:* Suzanne's mother, Grandma Sally, alters her sauce to include half strawberries and half raspberries, and she puts it through a sieve. "A sieve!" I exclaimed. "Who has time for that? The ice cream is waiting."

*old school:* If a food processor is not available, puree those berries with a handheld mixer or a potato masher.

# Tersey's Coffee Cake

*Submitted by Joanie Diener and Alison Rudolph Mayersohn*
*From Esther Rabinowitz (Rabwin) Feldman's recipe, Eveleth, Minnesota*

Esther Rabinowitz (later changed to Rabwin) was born in Chicago in 1893 to Jewish immigrants from the town of Tauragon, Lithuania. At some point, her family moved to the iron-rich mountain range of Eveleth, in northern Minnesota. They were part of a group of Eastern European Jewish immigrant families who lived in the range's small towns and owned stores that served the miners.

All of Esther's family, except one of her aunts, Tzvika, left Lithuania in the late nineteenth century. Tzvika stayed in Tauragon to take care of her parents (Esther's grandparents) and was killed along with most of the rest of her family by Nazis in the early stages of World War II. One of Tzvika's daughters, Shulamit, escaped and walked across Europe, hiding along the way until she finally made it to Israel. As far as her family knows, Esther only ever made one trip outside the United States—to visit her first cousin, Shulamit, in Israel in 1964.

After graduating from a Minnesota teachers college, Esther married Abe Feldman in 1914, and in 1927 they moved to Los Angeles. As the story goes, Esther became known as "Ter" because her young nieces and nephews could not pronounce "Aunt Esther." According to family lore, it was her son-in-law who changed it to "Tersey," and it endured. Tersey's grandchildren describe her as a beautiful woman who loved her family, *As the World Turns*, and the horse races. She and her husband went to the track whenever they could, and rumor has it she used a bookie when she couldn't get there!

Tersey made coffee cake for all occasions. In fact, if anyone in the family was going to a friend's house and needed to bring something, they just put in their order to Tersey and picked up the finished cake, often warm from the oven. The children considered it a big treat to help Tersey make the cake. Her granddaughter Alison recalled Tersey's "golden hands" and standing on the stool in Tersey's small kitchen, stirring the batter.

Tersey's granddaughter DeDe has that stool in her own kitchen today. DeDe spent every school vacation in Los Angeles visiting Tersey and Abe. After a long workweek, the family drove down the coast from the San Francisco Bay Area, usually arriving in the wee hours of the night. No matter what time they arrived, Tersey was always waiting for them with a fresh cake. DeDe says they began each morning of those vacations by snuggling under the covers with Tersey and eating coffee cake right there in bed! Grab your slippers and enjoy a slice.

{ *She and her husband went to the track whenever they could, and rumor has it she used a bookie when she couldn't get there!*

# Tersey's Coffee Cake MAKES 1 (9-INCH) SQUARE CAKE

**TOPPING**

½ cup granulated sugar

1 tablespoon ground cinnamon

**CAKE**

1¾ cups all-purpose flour

1½ teaspoons baking powder

1 teaspoon baking soda

⅛ teaspoon salt

½ cup (1 stick) butter, at room temperature

1 cup granulated sugar

2 large eggs

1 (8-ounce) container sour cream

Golden hands

Preheat the oven to 350°F. Butter and flour a 9-inch square baking dish (or use nonstick baking spray with flour) and set aside.

**To make the topping:** Place the sugar and cinnamon in a small bowl. Whisk or stir together and set aside.

**To make the cake:** In a medium bowl, whisk together the flour, baking powder, baking soda, and salt, and set aside. Place the butter and sugar in the bowl of a stand mixer fitted with the paddle attachment. Blend on medium speed until light and fluffy. Add the eggs, one at a time, mixing until each is incorporated. Add the sour cream and blend. With the mixer on low speed, blend in half of the dry ingredients until moistened. Add the remaining dry ingredients and blend until just combined.

Pour half the batter into the prepared pan. Sprinkle half of the cinnamon-sugar mixture over the batter, making sure to cover the surface evenly. Insert a knife into one end of the baking dish and gently swirl it through the batter from one end to the other. You want to ensure that the cinnamon mixture gets distributed through the cake, but don't overdo it—you're just swirling it through, not blending it. Pour the remaining batter on top and sprinkle the remaining cinnamon mixture over the batter. Bake for 35 to 45 minutes, until a toothpick inserted in the center comes out clean. Remove from the oven and let cool completely.

# Oh Me, Oh My, Carrot Cake

*Submitted by Sue Marguleas*
*From her grandmother Irene Gronemus Hammes's recipe, Middle Ridge, Wisconsin*

Irene Gronemus, born in 1917, was raised on a farm in Middle Ridge, Wisconsin. The oldest of five children, Irene was sent off at the age of 16 to cook for a family in La Crosse. There she met her future husband, Leo Hammes, and the married couple eventually returned to the countryside to raise a family and become dairy farmers. Irene had eight children, and cooking was a large part of her daily life. Delicious smells constantly wafted from her kitchen.

"Many of my grandmother's meals stand out in all of our minds as memorable, but her carrot cake is the favorite of all!" her granddaughter Sue told us. "I don't even think she knows where she got the recipe, but she has been making it for as long as any of us can remember and it always is delicious, even when she declares it a flop. It is at every family gathering, every reunion, every funeral, and she always has one in the freezer 'just in case.' All of us who have tried it say we can't make it as good as she does, but maybe it's because we don't want to, because if we do, she will stop, or because no one can ever replace her."

After raising her family, Irene once again took on a cooking role, preparing meals for retired nuns at a nearby convent. Her carrot cake is still requested by family and nuns alike. The recipe does not call for the typical cream cheese frosting, but rather for a traditional milk and flour version, such as our Classic Red Velvet Frosting, that Irene called simply "white frosting." It is the secret to the success of the cake.

{ *Her carrot cake is still requested by family and nuns alike.*

# Oh Me, Oh My, Carrot Cake MAKES 1 (9-INCH) ROUND LAYER CAKE

| | |
|---|---|
| 2 cups all-purpose flour | 4 large eggs |
| 2 teaspoons baking powder | 3 cups finely grated carrots (from 4 to 6 medium carrots) |
| 2 teaspoons baking soda | |
| 1 teaspoon salt | 1 cup finely chopped walnuts, divided (optional) |
| 2 teaspoons ground cinnamon | |
| 1½ cups granulated sugar | 1 batch Classic Red Velvet Frosting (page 23) |
| 1½ cups vegetable oil | Rosary beads |

Preheat the oven to 350°F. Butter and flour two 9-inch round cake pans (or use nonstick baking spray with flour) and set aside.

Place the flour, baking powder, baking soda, salt, and cinnamon in a medium bowl. Whisk together and set aside. In the bowl of a stand mixer fitted with the paddle attachment, mix the sugar and oil on medium speed until combined. Add the eggs, one at a time, blending on low speed until each is incorporated. Add half of the dry ingredients and mix on low speed until just incorporated. Add the second half of the dry ingredients, mixing on low speed until the dry ingredients are moist. Use a spatula to fold in the carrots and, if desired, ½ cup of the nuts. Mix until just combined.

Pour the batter into the prepared pans and spread it evenly. Bake for 25 to 30 minutes, until a toothpick inserted in the center comes out clean. Remove from the oven and cool the cakes in the pans on top of wire racks for 10 minutes, then carefully turn the cakes out onto the wire racks and let cool completely.

Place one cooled cake layer upside down on a serving platter and use a knife or an angled spatula to spread frosting over the top and sides, being generous on top, as it will be a filling layer. Place the next layer right side up on top of the first and complete the frosting of the top and sides. Top with the remaining chopped nuts, if desired.

_notes_

_carpool crunch:_ Buy grated carrots and chopped walnuts at the market. Or use a food processor fitted with a shredding or grating attachment to grate the carrots or a chopping blade to grind the nuts.

_modern variation:_ Use Hummingbird Cream Cheese Frosting (page 14) and top with chopped nuts, if desired. This frosting recipe may be doubled if, like us, you indulge in eating the frosting while decorating the cake.

_sass it up:_ This recipe is very versatile. Irene used a 9 by 13-inch baking dish because she had many mouths to feed. If you want to be impressive and don't mind a bit more labor, use three round cake pans. Just split the batter evenly among the pans and don't forget to adjust your baking time if using a pan different from the one specified. If you want to bring a treat to school or work, you can even try making carrot cake muffins. See our Cake Pan Volume Conversion Chart (page 274) for guidance.

_sugar mommas note:_ We prefer to use nuts sparingly as a decoration on the frosting so that we can discreetly pick around them without looking tacky.

# Coconut Angel Food Cake

*Submitted by Catherine Watson*
*From her grandmother Luta Frierson Keith's recipe, Anderson, South Carolina*

Catherine Watson fondly recalls her grandmother Luta Frierson Keith, who was born in 1892 and was affectionately known as Ma-Ma. Everything Ma-Ma made was heavenly, but this cake was Catherine's favorite. "Ma-Ma appeared at the door every Christmas morning wearing her wispy little hat, leather gloves, and that mink tail 'thingie' around her suit . . . you know the kind where the mouth opens and hooks to a tail? She carried that mile-high cake, looking just like one of the Wise Men!"

Catherine reminisces, "Tell me grandmothers don't make major memories for the little ones. I am over 60 and it's as if it were yesterday." Now Catherine carries on Ma-Ma's tradition and makes Coconut Angel Food Cake every Christmas. When we asked Catherine to share a recipe with us, she wrote to Momma Reiner, "I have decided, Kimberly, that this is really fun! So many happy memories seem to revolve around food . . . especially sweets . . . and typing these recipes off reminded me of how often I have made them and all the calories that went out my front door!!"

{ *"Ma-Ma appeared at the door every Christmas morning wearing her wispy little hat, leather gloves, and that mink tail 'thingie' around her suit . . ."*

# Coconut Angel Food Cake MAKES 1 LAYERED CAKE

1    cup all-purpose flour

1    teaspoon cream of tartar

11   large egg whites

1½   cups granulated sugar

¼    teaspoon vanilla extract

1    batch Angel Food White Icing
     (recipe follows)

2 to 3 cups sweetened flaked coconut
     (Catherine uses Baker's Angel
     Flake)

Mink tail thingie

Preheat the oven to 325°F.

In a medium bowl, whisk together the flour and cream of tartar. Set aside. In the bowl of a stand mixer fitted with the whisk attachment, beat the egg whites until stiff but not dry, about 1½ minutes. (Ma-Ma's directions say to whip those egg whites sky-high!) Use a spatula to slowly fold the sugar into the egg whites. Do not beat. Add the vanilla. Add the flour mixture into the egg whites, a little at a time, stirring gently. Pour the batter evenly into an ungreased standard angel food cake pan. Bake for about 50 minutes, until the cake springs back when touched in the center. Gently invert the pan and set on a wire rack to cool completely. You may also invert the pan on top of a bottle (neck through the hole of your tube pan) to allow the cake to cool. While the cake is cooling, make the icing.

Slice the cooled cake into three layers. Place one cake layer upside down on a serving platter and spread icing over the top and sides, being generous on top, as it will be a filling layer. Cover the icing with coconut. Place the middle layer upside down on top of the bottom layer, spread icing over the top and sides, again, being generous with the top/filling layer, and sprinkle coconut over it. Place the third cake layer right side up on top of the second layer and complete the frosting of the top and sides. Sprinkle the remaining coconut over the entire cake, covering it evenly.

*notes*

## SUGAR MOMMAS TIPS

*sugar mommas nifty gadget:* Use Wilton's egg separator to obtain fast and easy egg whites with no mess. The egg yolk sits in a top cavity while the whites slip through slots into a bottom compartment. This is fun to watch, and the kids get a kick out of it.

*old school:* If you can't find flaked coconut, you may use sweetened shredded coconut. Luta used one fresh coconut, which she shredded herself. This seems like a perfect excuse for a Hawaiian vacation.

*carpool crunch:* If you're rushing off to a function and want to bring an impressive cake, look no further. No need to slice into layers and frost individually. Just take the whole cake out of the tube pan, frost the top and sides, sprinkle with coconut (you'll only need about 1½ cups), and serve.

*sass it up:* Vanilla extract can be used in place of almond for the icing. You can also add sliced fruit between your layers. Try adding a few drops of blue or red food coloring to the icing for a petal pink or sky blue cake—perfect for a baby shower.

## Angel Food White Icing

Note: You will need a candy thermometer for this recipe.

- 1½ cups granulated sugar
- ½ teaspoon cream of tartar
- ⅛ teaspoon salt
- ½ cup hot water
- ½ cup egg whites (from about 4 large eggs, separated)
- ¼ teaspoon almond extract

In a saucepan over medium heat, mix together the sugar, cream of tartar, salt, and hot water. Bring to a boil, stirring constantly until the sugar is dissolved (the liquid should change from cloudy to clear), 3 to 5 minutes. Cover the saucepan and boil for about 1 minute to wash down any sugar crystals that may have formed on the sides of the saucepan. Remove the lid. Continue to cook without stirring until a candy thermometer reads 240°F. Remove from the heat and allow it to cool just a bit.

When the candy thermometer reads 236°F, beat the egg whites in the bowl of a stand mixer fitted with the whisk attachment on medium to high speed until stiff peaks form, about 4 minutes. Add the sugar syrup slowly to the egg whites, beating on medium speed. Add the almond extract and continue to beat for 5 to 8 minutes, until the frosting is cool and holds its shape.

CHAPTER
3

tarts and pies
worth the lie

Have these thoughts ever crossed your mind? "Bake a pie? It's too hard. I don't have the supplies, or the time. I don't know how to make a crust. What if the crust isn't flaky? I don't know how to crimp. Can't I just buy a pie at the store?" Fear not! We have insight.

- There are only four ingredients in a basic pie crust.

- It takes less time to make a crust from scratch than it does to drive to the store, or to even think about thawing a frozen one.

- In a pinch, ready-made pie crusts are available everywhere.

Once you get the hang of it, you can sass up your shell by adding sugar, vanilla, lemon zest, almond extract, nuts, or other ingredients that tickle your fancy. If you have the slightest creative spark, you will love all that you can do with crimping and fluting. Pie pans exist with fluted edges built in. All you have to do is mold your dough to the pan. Presto! Your crust will look professional. Think of your kitchen as a laboratory and an experiment. Even an ugly pie will taste amazing.

Many of the pies throughout this chapter came to us with their own crust recipes. Though some are similar, none is exactly the same. If you find one you like—it flakes or crumbles just right, you find it easy to work with, it tastes delicious—then by all means, stick with it.

Think of the dough as adult Play-Doh. Bend it, roll it, shape it, and make a ball. When your crust is ready to be filled, imagine it oozing with something buttery, dripping with fruits and berries, filled with sassy tangy sweetness, or thick with finger-licking pudding. Turn the page and give it a go.

# Annabelle's Puddin' Pies

*Submitted by Momma Jenna*
*From her grandmother Ann Pinto's recipe, Milford, Connecticut*

Gram's given name was Ann but her younger brothers always called her Annabelle (Italian for "beautiful Ann"), and it stuck. She was married at 16, had four daughters by the age of 25, and spent the better part of early adulthood cooking for her family. When Annabelle became a grandmother ("Grandma Belles"), she earned the right to bake for enjoyment. One of Gram's greatest joys was baking for her grandchildren.

I had the privilege of living with Grandma Belles while I attended college in Connecticut. As a young student far away from home, I felt treasured when Gram cooked one of her elaborate meals on my behalf. She taught me that cooking for loved ones is a pleasure. Watching me enjoy a piece of pie brought Gram pure satisfaction.

After four years I got accustomed to Gram's cooking. By that time, every dessert had been refined to perfection. I occasionally followed her around the kitchen like an apprentice to learn her techniques, and she revealed her secrets to me. I asked if one day I could have her recipe book because it held so many cherished recipes and memories. Gram was delighted by my request.

A few years later Gram passed away unexpectedly. Family heirlooms and modest jewelry were doled out to her children. Gram's cookbook remained with Aunt Lynda, who made copies for my mother and her two other sisters. Months later, a package arrived in the mail. Upon opening the box, I found Gram's cookbook. Lynda had made herself a copy and sent me the original.

Today that collection of recipes is my most cherished possession. *Grandma's Recipes* etched in the cover, it is a compilation of delicacies written in her own hand. Its value is so much greater than the individual ingredients and instructions it contains. The book is a lifetime of love, expressed through a bit of butter, flour, and sugar.

Rather than appetizers or entrées, Grandma Belles began her handwritten cookbook with pies. Clearly the apple doesn't fall far from the family tree. I am particularly fond of her chocolate and vanilla cream pies. They are so rich, creamy, and *decadent*. Each bite reminds me of sitting at the kitchen table talking and laughing, playing cribbage or poker, and hanging out like girlfriends. I can still see every detail of that modest kitchen in my mind. Gram was a blast. She had a hearty sense of humor and an infectious laugh.

I am delighted to share Gram's scrumptious pies with you. Let's begin with her no-fail crust. Grab the rolling pin and some flour.

{ *The book is a lifetime of love, expressed through a bit of butter, flour, and sugar.*

## Annabelle's
## Basic Single Pie Shell
**(MOMMA JENNA'S PREFERRED PIE CRUST)**

1½   cups all-purpose flour

½   teaspoon salt

½   cup vegetable shortening

4 to 5 tablespoons ice-cold water

Preheat the oven to 425°F. In a large bowl, stir together the flour and salt with a fork. Add the shortening and cut in using only your fork—no hands!—until the dough forms pieces the size of small peas. Slowly add the water, 1 tablespoon at a time, and mix with the fork. Use just enough water to make a soft dough that holds together. Start with the 4 tablespoons, and add 1 more tablespoon if necessary, but too much water will make the dough sticky.

Shape the dough into a ball with your hands, but do not handle it excessively. Roll the dough out on a lightly floured surface until it is about 14 inches in diameter and ⅛ inch thick. You should have enough to cover a 9-inch pie plate, with ½ inch or so overlapping the edge. Transfer the dough to a pie dish (see Sugar Mommas Notes) and gently press it against the bottom and sides. Flute the edge (see Sugar Mommas Notes). Use a fork to prick small holes in the bottom and sides of the dough to prevent puffing.

Bake for 11 to 13 minutes, until lightly golden, checking halfway through to see if the crust is puffing up. If so, prick it again with the fork. Remove from the oven and let cool completely.

## SUGAR MOMMAS TIPS

*sugar mommas notes:* To transfer dough without overhandling, roll the dough around your rolling pin and then "unroll" it into the pie plate. If you have overhang, tuck the dough under the inside edge of the plate.

To flute easily and uniformly, use the handle of a wooden spoon. Holding the spoon in your right hand, tuck the end of the handle under the edge of the dough, then press both sides of the dough down over the top of the spoon handle with the thumb and forefinger of your left hand. Move the handle over slightly and repeat as you rotate the plate with your left hand.

See a video demonstration on www. SugarSugarRecipes.com.

*carpool crunch:* This dough may be prepared in advance. After you shape the dough into a ball, cover with plastic wrap, then seal in a plastic freezer bag or other airtight container. It will keep in the freezer for up to 2 weeks. Thaw in the refrigerator the night before the crust is to be used. Then roll it out and bake as instructed in the recipe.

# Chocolate Puddin' Pie MAKES 1 (9-INCH) PIE

¾ cup granulated sugar

½ teaspoon salt

5 tablespoons cornstarch

2½ cups whole milk

2 ounces unsweetened chocolate, melted

3 egg yolks

1 teaspoon vanilla extract

Annabelle's Basic Single Pie Shell (page 69) or 1 ready-made 9-inch pie crust, prebaked and cooled completely

1 batch Annabelle's Whipped Cream Topping (recipe follows)

Bells

Place the sugar, salt, and cornstarch in a large saucepan over medium heat. Gradually stir in the milk and then the chocolate. Using a spoon, stir constantly to prevent sticking. The chocolate will separate into a million tiny flakes in the milk mixture but will eventually smooth out. Continue stirring until the mixture begins to thicken, about 15 minutes. The consistency should be like a thick cream soup. In a small bowl, whisk the egg yolks. To temper the eggs, pour about 1 cup of the hot, thickened milk mixture into the bowl of yolks. Quickly whisk them together and then slowly blend the egg mixture back into the hot milk in the saucepan. Decrease the heat to low and cook for 2 minutes longer, stirring constantly, until the mixture takes on the consistency of pudding. Remove from the heat and stir in the vanilla.

Allow the filling to cool in the pan for 5 minutes, stirring occasionally to prevent a skin from forming. Pour the filling into the cooled crust and chill for at least 1 hour. Top with the whipped cream topping and serve.

## Annabelle's Whipped Cream Topping

1   cup heavy whipping cream

½   cup confectioners' sugar

½   teaspoon vanilla extract

In the bowl of a stand mixer fitted with the whisk attachment, whip the cream on high speed until it begins to stiffen. Add the sugar and vanilla and beat until stiff peaks form.

*notes*

*sugar mommas note:* To melt chocolate easily without wrestling with a double boiler, place the chocolate in a glass or other microwave-safe bowl and heat on high power for 30-second intervals, stirring in between each interval to avoid burning.

*sass it up:* Use European chocolate, such as Valrhona or Guittard, available at most markets or specialty stores.

Add one or two capfuls of your favorite liqueur in lieu of vanilla in the whipped cream topping.

*modern variation:* We prefer a less sweet version of whipped cream with only a tablespoon or two of granualted sugar.

# Vanilla Puddin' Pie MAKES 1 (9-INCH) PIE

⅔ cup granulated sugar

½ teaspoon salt

6 tablespoons cornstarch

3 cups whole milk

3 egg yolks

1 tablespoon butter, at room temperature

1½ teaspoons vanilla extract

Annabelle's Basic Single Pie Shell (page 69) or 1 ready-made 9-inch pie crust, prebaked and cooled completely

1 batch Annabelle's Whipped Cream Topping (page 71; optional)

Treasured hand-me-down

Place the sugar, salt, and cornstarch in a large saucepan over medium heat. Gradually stir in the milk and cook, stirring constantly, until the mixture begins to thicken, 11 to 14 minutes. The consistency should be like a thick cream soup. In a small bowl, whisk the egg yolks. To temper the eggs, pour about 1 cup of the hot, thickened milk mixture into the bowl of yolks. Quickly whisk them together and then slowly blend the egg mixture back into the hot milk in your saucepan. Decrease the heat to low and cook for 2 minutes longer, stirring constantly, until the mixture takes on the consistency of pudding. Remove from the heat. Stir in the butter until melted, then mix in the vanilla.

Allow the filling to cool in the pan for 5 minutes, stirring occasionally to prevent a skin from forming. Pour the filling into the cooled crust and chill for at least 1 hour. Serve alone or topped with the whipped cream topping.

**Banana Puddin' Pie:** Momma Jenna slices bananas onto the bottom of the baked crust before filling it with vanilla cream. Momma Reiner dices up bananas to layer all over and in between! For an updated twist, try it in a pecan crust (see El's Butterscotch Pie, page 76).

**Coconut Puddin' Pie:** After the vanilla cream mixture has cooled, fold ¾ cup sweetened shredded coconut into the filling before pouring it into the baked crust. Decorate by sprinkling toasted coconut on top. Serve alone or topped with whipped cream.

# El's Butterscotch Pie

*Submitted by Helen Levin*
*From her grandmother Eleanor Hutchison's recipe, Abilene, Texas*

Helen decided to create a family cookbook, so she began rummaging through old recipes. Somewhere amidst note cards, clippings, and scribbled slips of paper—many on the backs of checks, and even one on the Abilene public school schedule—Helen came across this recipe. When she asked her relatives to share any memories they had about Grandma El (pronounced EEL) and her butterscotch pie, the responses varied. Cousin Helen (whom our contributor was named after) remembered Eleanor as a smart woman, a great manager, funny as hell, but *not* a good cook. Cousin Sarah, on the other hand, said, "Butterscotch pie? I thought it was Scotch pie! Growing up, I figured it was for John A. [because he drank Scotch], so I never ate it!"

We are here to announce to all of Helen's relatives, old and young, that this butterscotch pie is a winner. The pecan crust is a pleasant surprise when you bite into it, contrasting with the mellow butterscotch filling. You may want to resurrect El's recipe and add it to the rotation. Your family and friends will think you invented something new. Accept the praise and offer up another slice.

{ *"Butterscotch pie? I thought it was Scotch pie . . . so I never ate it!"*

# El's Butterscotch Pie MAKES 1 (9-INCH) PIE

## PECAN CRUST

1    cup all-purpose flour

¼    cup packed light brown sugar

½    cup chopped pecans

½    cup (1 stick) butter, cold, cut into thin slices

## BUTTERSCOTCH FILLING

1    cup packed light brown sugar

⅓    cup all-purpose flour

½    teaspoon salt

2    cups whole milk

2    egg yolks

2    tablespoons butter, at room temperature

½    teaspoon vanilla extract

1    batch Sugar Mommas Rum Cream Topping (recipe follows) or Annabelle's Whipped Cream Topping (page 71)

Glass of Scotch

**To make the crust:** Preheat the oven to 350°F. Place the flour, brown sugar, and pecans in the bowl of a food processor. Pulse a few times to mix. Add the butter and pulse several times until it is well incorporated and the mixture forms moist crumbs. Press the mixture firmly and evenly in the bottom and up the sides of a 9-inch pie plate. Bake for about 20 minutes, until the crust begins to turn golden in the center. Remove from the oven and set aside to let cool.

**To make the filling:** Place the sugar, flour, and salt in a large saucepan over medium heat. Gradually stir in the milk and continue stirring for 8 to 10 minutes, until the mixture begins to thicken. The consistency should be like a thick cream soup. In a small bowl, whisk the egg yolks. To temper the eggs, pour about 1 cup of the hot, thickened milk mixture into the bowl of yolks. Quickly whisk together and then slowly blend the egg mixture back into the hot milk in your saucepan, stirring continuously. Decrease the heat to low and cook for 1 minute longer, stirring constantly, until the mixture takes on the consistency of pudding. Remove from the heat. Stir in the butter until melted, then stir in the vanilla. Allow the filling to cool in the pan for about 5 minutes, stirring occasionally to prevent a skin from forming. Pour the filling into the cooled crust and chill for 4 hours to overnight. Serve alone or topped with the Rum Cream Topping that follows.

## Sugar Mommas
## Rum Cream Topping

1   cup heavy whipping cream

1   tablespoon granulated sugar

2   capfuls rum

In the bowl of a stand mixer fitted with the whisk attachment, whip the cream on high speed until it begins to stiffen. Add the sugar and rum and beat until soft peaks form.

*notes*

## SUGAR MOMMAS TIPS

*sass it up:* Go a little "nuts" and sprinkle some chopped pecans on top of the pie.

# Cooks and Kooks Key Lime Pie

*Submitted by Marie Warren Fayz*
*From her mother Anna Rose McDonald Warren's recipe, Nashville, Tennessee*

Anna Rose's family originated in Scotland (paternal) and Ireland (maternal), immigrated to Virginia in the 1600s, and eventually settled in Tennessee. Always a tight-knit clan—Clanranald from the Scottish Highlands—they still have reunions twice yearly.

Anna Rose was born in 1925, the middle child of 11 McDonald children. She grew up in the rural town of Monterey, Tennessee, located midway between Nashville and Knoxville on the Cumberland Plateau. As in many small communities across the country at that time, there was not much entertainment for the children, so they amused themselves the best they could. Anna Rose and her sisters would sit upstairs in their house during the hot, humid Tennessee summers (no air-conditioning, of course) and make paper dolls by cutting out models from a Sears, Roebuck catalog.

From their bedroom window, the girls could see the town's cemetery. Whenever they saw a procession heading up from the funeral home for a graveside service, they would throw down their paper dolls, grab their brothers, and run over like blue blazes to the cemetery to watch the burial. It didn't matter if they had no idea who the deceased person was.

When the kids were not chasing after dead people, there was a lot of cooking to be done. Each child had assigned chores, and many of them grew up to be skilled cooks and bakers. Anna Rose was no exception. In 1938, the family moved to Nashville, where Anna Rose met her husband in high school. In the early years of their marriage, her husband joked that she cooked meals big enough for 10 people.

Once Anna Rose had a family of her own, they vacationed in Florida. She fell in love with the tropical weather and the key lime pie. Anna Rose made the pie when she returned home because it was a light and refreshing dessert in the oppressive Southern heat.

Her daughter Marie shared this recipe with us. Now, every time Marie takes a bite of this pie she thinks of childhood vacations and her family—especially her mother, Anna Rose. Marie says there are many "cooks and kooks" in her clan. We can certainly relate to that.

{ *When the kids were not chasing after dead people, there was a lot of cooking to be done.*

# Cooks and Kooks Key Lime Pie MAKES 1 (9-INCH) PIE

**GRAHAM CRACKER CRUST**

1½  cups graham cracker crumbs

¼   cup (½ stick) butter, melted

**FILLING**

2   eggs yolks (reserve the whites for the meringue topping)

1   (14-ounce) can sweetened condensed milk

½   cup fresh key lime juice (from about 16 key limes)

*Braveheart* DVD

**MERINGUE TOPPING**

2   egg whites

2   tablespoons granulated sugar

**To make the crust:** Preheat the oven to 350°F. Place the graham cracker crumbs in the bowl of a food processor. While the machine is on, add the melted butter. Pulse several times until the mixture forms moist crumbs. Press the mixture firmly and evenly in the bottom and up the sides of a 9-inch pie dish and set aside. The crust will set when it is chilled with the filling inside.

**To make the filling:** Place the egg yolks in the bowl of a stand mixer fitted with the paddle attachment and beat on high speed until light and creamy, about 1 minute. Reduce the speed to medium and blend in the condensed milk. Use a spatula to fold in the key lime juice. Pour the filling into the crust.

**To make the meringue topping:** Place the egg whites in the bowl of a stand mixer fitted with the whisk attachment and beat on high speed until foamy. Reduce the speed to medium and slowly add the sugar and mix until the egg whites are glossy. Spoon the meringue on top of the pie filling, making sure to cover the top completely. Bake for 10 to 15 minutes, until the meringue is slightly browned. Remove from the oven and set aside to let cool at room temperature for 30 minutes. Chill in the refrigerator before serving.

*notes*

_____

_____

_____

_____

_____

_____

_____

_____

_____

_____

_____

_____

_____

_____

_____

_____

_____

## SUGAR MOMMAS TIPS

*old school:* If you don't have a food processor, place the graham crackers inside a large, resealable plastic bag and crush with a rolling pin or meat mallet. Pour the crumbs into a mixing bowl, stir in the melted butter, and mix until a coarse meal forms. Press the mixture firmly and evenly in the bottom and up the sides of the pie pan.

*carpool crunch:* If you're pressed for time or feeling super-lazy, buy a ready-made graham cracker crust.

To speed your filling prep, dust off your electric juicer and put it to good use. You can also use bottled lime juice, but make certain it is from key limes. We recommend the brand Nellie & Joe's.

*sugar mommas note:* You can top this pie with whipped cream instead of meringue, such as Annabelle's Whipped Cream Topping (page 71). In that case, there is no need to bake it. It is more authentic unbaked—as they say in the South, "The lime does the cookin'!" Technically, the lime doesn't actually cook the eggs (if you want to get scientific, it denatures them). If topping with whipped cream (either store-bought or homemade) in lieu of meringue, simply spoon the whipped cream on top of the cooled pie filling and chill before serving.

# Lucinda Bell's $100 Pecan Pie

*Submitted by Zeita Parker Jones*
*From her nanny Lucinda Bell's recipe, Jackson, Mississippi*

Lucinda Bell had many talents, but her forte was cooking. She was renowned throughout Jackson, Mississippi, for her pecan pie. Lucinda's employer, Mr. Parker, was an attorney recognized in the community for his honesty and integrity. But every man has his weakness. Mr. Parker's was Lucinda's pie.

A descendant of slaves and sharecroppers, Lucinda spent the greater part of her life picking cotton in the sweltering Mississippi heat. She had ten children, the youngest five of whom were born while Lucinda harvested cotton on a plantation. Lucinda remembers giving birth to a baby, placing him in a sling, and going back to working the field. When her youngest child was 10 years old, Lucinda was ready for less arduous labor, and began working for the Parkers.

Zeita has many fond memories of her nanny, who worked in the family's home for 35 years. Zeita often skipped school to stay home with Lucinda, whom she referred to as her "second mom." She would sit on the dryer while Lucinda did laundry, and become immersed in Lucinda's vivid history lessons about slavery. Zeita soaked up every word of Lucinda's thoughts about growing up black in the South. Although Lucinda had little formal education and could not read or write, she taught Zeita volumes about life.

Mr. Parker appreciated Lucinda's care for his daughter, and he particularly enjoyed Lucinda's culinary skills. Mr. Parker frequently hid $100 bills around the house, a fact Lucinda knew well. As Lucinda baked in their kitchen, Mr. Parker would nonchalantly ask her if she had made any extra pies. "How many $100s you got?" Lucinda quipped. He wryly replied, "How many pies do you have?" as he slipped her a crisp $100 bill.

Lucinda informed Zeita that she made three pies at a time—one each for Mr. Parker, Mrs. Parker, and Zeita. Mr. Parker repeatedly told his daughter that Lucinda only baked two pies, though Lucinda swore she had cooked three. Zeita assumed Lucinda's mind was getting a little fuzzy with age. That third pie remained elusive.

Years later, Lucinda was cleaning out Mr. Parker's closet when pie tins began tumbling onto her head from the top shelf. When Zeita ran to see what all the ruckus was about, imagine her shock to discover that her "honest Abe" daddy had been secretly stashing and eating the third pie! Zeita planned to confront her father when he returned home from work. Given that Mr. Parker was diabetic, it was particularly alarming to Zeita when he told her he wouldn't give up his pie—he'd just take more insulin!

Zeita tells us that visitors dropped by the Parker residence hoping to get a slice. However, Mr. Parker didn't give up his pie easily. He could be overheard in the kitchen purposely saying in a loud, discouraging voice, "Can't you just give them a cookie?"

This recipe had never been written down before . . . until now. Zeita shadowed Lucinda in the kitchen to capture the measurements and transcribe the directions. Every time we take a bite, we honor Lucinda Bell.

{ *Lucinda was cleaning out Mr. Parker's closet when pie tins began tumbling onto her head from the top shelf.*

# Lucinda Bell's $100 Pecan Pie MAKES 1 (9-INCH) PIE

1 single-crust pie shell from this chapter or 1 ready-made 9-inch pie crust, unbaked

1 cup granulated sugar

¼ cup (½ stick) butter, at room temperature

3 large eggs

1 cup light corn syrup

1 teaspoon vanilla extract

1 cup chopped pecans

Cookies for guests so you don't have to share your pie

Preheat the oven to 350°F. Place the rolled-out pie dough in a 9-inch pie plate and flute the edges (see Sugar Mommas Note, page 69).

Place the sugar and butter in the bowl of a stand mixer fitted with the paddle attachment and beat on medium speed until light and fluffy. Reduce the speed to low and add the eggs, one at a time, mixing just until each is incorporated. Add the corn syrup and vanilla extract. Use a wooden spoon or spatula to fold in the pecans. Pour the filling into the pie shell and bake for 45 to 50 minutes. According to Lucinda, "just keep checkin' it" until it's done (Sugar Mommas Interpretation: until the pie filling is firm and no longer jiggles in the center). Remove from the oven and set aside to cool completely before cutting.

*notes* _____

_____

_____

_____

_____

_____

{ *Classic and simple, this is the perfect pecan pie! The color is spot-on. The texture and taste leave you begging for more.*

# Fourth of July Apple Pie

*Submitted by Celia "Muffy" Hunt*
*From her grandmother Ida Vaughan's recipe, Urbana, Missouri*

Muffy's grandmother Ida Vaughan kept the kids busy on the family farm during the 1940s. Muffy remembers that one of the chores was making butter in a crank-style churn. We think that alone should have earned her first dibs on a slice of pie.

Fireworks were probably all the rage in post—World War II American cities, but in rural Missouri, Independence Day was a time filled with food. Muffy's family always made apple pie for Fourth of July picnics. "I don't think I ever saw fireworks on the Fourth until after I was married," she contends. To this day, Muffy would rather make her pie than any other dessert. She also suggests serving it at a dinner party to be certain it is consumed all at once. Otherwise you may end up eating it yourself.

It wasn't easy for Muffy to pin Grandma Ida down for her recipe. Like so many women we have known, Ida used "a pinch of this, and a spoonful of that." Muffy was finally able to convince Ida to measure out some of her recipes so they could be recorded. At 103, she was passing out the apple pie recipe to her caretakers. Ida lived to 104, but her apple pie lives on and on.

{ *At 103, she was passing out the apple pie recipe to her caretakers.*

## Fourth of July
## Double-Crust Pie Dough

| | |
|---|---|
| 2 | cups all-purpose flour |
| ½ | teaspoon baking powder |
| ¾ | teaspoon salt |
| 6 | tablespoons (¾ stick) butter, chilled and cut into thin slices |
| 6 | tablespoons vegetable shortening |

4 to 6 tablespoons ice-cold water

Place the flour, baking powder, and salt in the bowl of a food processor. Pulse a few times to mix. Add the butter and shortening. Pulse 10 to 15 times, until the mixture forms small nuggets. Pour the mixture into a large bowl. Add the cold water, 1 tablespoon at a time, using a fork to mix it until the mixture holds together.

Carefully turn out the dough onto parchment paper and shape it into a ball. Divide it roughly in half, wrap each half in plastic wrap or parchment paper, and chill for at least 1 hour or up to overnight.

# Fourth of July Apple Pie MAKES 1 (9-INCH) PIE

1    cup granulated sugar

1    teaspoon ground cinnamon

½    teaspoon ground nutmeg

2    tablespoons all-purpose flour, divided

6 or 7 Granny Smith apples, cored, peeled, and sliced

1    batch Fourth of July Double-Crust Pie Dough

1    tablespoon butter, cut into small pieces

Fireworks

Preheat the oven to 425°F. In a small bowl, whisk together the sugar, cinnamon, nutmeg, and 1 tablespoon of the flour. Place the apples in a large bowl. Sprinkle the sugar mixture over them and toss to coat.

Roll out half of the chilled pie dough on a lightly floured work surface until it is 14 inches in diameter and ⅛ inch thick (large enough to fill your 9-inch pie plate and leave ½ to 1 inch hanging over the edges). Loosely roll the dough around the rolling pin, then unroll it into the pie plate and press gently against the bottom and sides.

Sprinkle the remaining 1 tablespoon flour over the bottom pie crust. Pour the apple mixture into the crust. Dot evenly with the butter. Roll out the second half of the dough to about 10 inches in diameter. Gently cover the apple mixture with the top pastry. Crimp the edges by pinching together lightly (use a bit of water to moisten the bottom crust if needed to help adhere it to the top crust). Make three 1-inch slits in the top crust to allow steam to escape.

Bake for 15 minutes at 425°F, then decrease the heat to 350°F and bake for 45 minutes longer, or until the crust turns golden and the juices begin to bubble. Remove from the oven and set aside to cool.

## notes

_____

_____

_____

_____

_____

_____

_____

_____

_____

_____

_____

_____

_____

_____

## SUGAR MOMMAS TIPS

*sugar mommas note:* If you find the edges are browning too quickly, use a pie shield, or cover the edges of the crust with aluminum foil. Remove the foil for the last 10 minutes of baking.

*sass it up:* For a light golden crust, use a pastry brush to coat the dough lightly with 2 tablespoons of milk just before baking. For a light golden glaze, brush with 1 beaten egg white. For a darker golden glaze, brush with a mixture made from whisking 1 whole egg with 1 tablespoon water.

# Cape Cod Blueberry Pie

*Submitted by Anne Blomstrom*
*From her mother Alethia King Stevens's recipe, Cape Cod, Massachusetts*

Every summer Anne Blomstrom's city-dwelling family made the trek from Chicago to visit her mother, Alethia, on Cape Cod. Thoughts of winter instantly melted away at the sight of the shingled white house trimmed with green shutters. For a few weeks in June and July, Anne's children would pick wild berries with their grandmother. At the time, blueberries were not readily available in the market, so this was a summertime activity everyone looked forward to.

Once the berries were collected, Alethia performed magic and created her blueberry pie. After supper, the family sat at the handcrafted picnic table in their front yard, enjoying the crisp, salty New England breeze and mouthfuls of pie, hot and bubbly from the oven. As the fork broke the crust and blueberry juice trickled out onto the fresh vanilla ice cream from the local creamery, the kids quietly listened as Alethia read *Blueberries for Sal* in honor of the treat they shared.

{ *After supper, the family sat . . . enjoying the crisp, salty New England breeze and mouthfuls of pie, hot and bubbly from the oven.*

## Cape Cod
## Double-Crust Pie Dough
**(MOMMA REINER'S PREFERRED PIE CRUST)**

| | |
|---|---|
| 2½ | cups all-purpose flour |
| 1 | teaspoon granulated sugar |
| 1 | teaspoon salt |
| 1 | cup (2 sticks) butter, cold, cut into thin slices |
| ⅓ | cup ice-cold water |

Place the flour, sugar, and salt in the bowl of a food processor. Pulse a few times to mix. Add the butter. Pulse 10 to 15 times, until the mixture resembles coarse meal. Add the water by the spoonful while pulsing until the mixture holds together (not more than 30 seconds).

Carefully turn out the dough onto parchment paper and shape it into a ball. Divide it roughly in half, wrap each half in plastic wrap or parchment paper, and chill for at least 1 hour or up to overnight.

*notes*

*carpool crunch:* Decide who the pie is for—the kids or the company? For the kids, buy ready-made pie dough. If you're having company, call ahead and order fancy pie dough from the gourmet food store or your local bakery.

*sugar mommas note:* This filling thickens the day after baking and has the perfect consistency. If you want to eat it right out of the oven, go for it, but it is very juicy. We suggest adding 1 to 2 tablespoons cornstarch to your dry ingredients when whisking them together in the bowl. This will prevent the berry nectar from being too runny.

*modern variation:* Make this pie with any edible berry growing in your backyard—lingonberry, huckleberry, gooseberry, elderberry—but please make sure it is safe for consumption!

# Cape Cod Blueberry Pie MAKES 1 (9-INCH) PIE

1 cup minus 1 tablespoon granulated sugar, divided

3 tablespoons all-purpose flour

¼ teaspoon salt

4 cups (about 24 ounces) wild blueberries (or cultivated berries if wild are not within reach)

1 batch Cape Cod Double-Crust Pie Dough

2 tablespoons fresh lemon juice

2 tablespoons butter, cut into small pieces

1 tablespoon whole milk

Vanilla ice cream, for serving

*Blueberries for Sal* by Robert McCloskey

Preheat the oven to 400°F. Set aside 1 tablespoon of the sugar for topping the pie. In a small bowl, whisk together the remaining sugar, the flour, and salt. Set aside. Place the berries in a large bowl, sprinkle the sugar mixture over them, and toss to coat.

Roll out half of the chilled dough on a lightly floured work surface until it is about 14 inches in diameter and ⅛ inch thick (large enough to fill your 9-inch pie plate and leave ½ to 1 inch hanging over the edges). Loosely roll the dough around the rolling pin, then unroll it into a pie plate and press gently against the bottom and sides.

Fill the pie shell with the berry mixture. Pour the lemon juice over the top. Dot evenly with the butter. Roll out the second half of the dough to about 10 inches in diameter. Cover the filling with the dough and crimp the edges by pinching together lightly (use a bit of water to moisten the bottom crust if needed to help it adhere to the top crust). Use a pastry brush to glaze the top crust with the milk. Sprinkle the remaining 1 tablespoon of sugar on top. Make three 1-inch slits in the top crust to allow steam to escape during baking. Cover the edges of the crust with foil to prevent overbrowning.

Bake for 40 minutes. Remove the foil from the crust edges and continue baking for 5 to 10 minutes longer, until the top crust is lightly browned and the fruit is bubbly. Remove from the oven and set aside to let cool. Serve with vanilla ice cream.

# Grasshopper Pie

*Submitted by Sandi Nutt*
*From her grandmother Helen Venturi's recipe, Plainville, Connecticut*

According to Sandi, Granny Helen was a natural cook but did not pass on her culinary talents to her daughter Eileen (Sandi's mother). Dad did the cooking in Sandi's family. However, there are some things only a mom can do . . . like mend a broken heart. The only time Eileen ventured into the kitchen was to create her cure-all elixir, grasshopper pie. The pie, with its bright green filling, was sure to produce a giggle and a smile. It never failed to cheer up the children when their spirits needed lifting.

Sandi recalls that the pie appeared when she did not make the cheerleading squad. It also materialized when a boy broke up with her in high school. Sandi ate the entire pie! We've all been there.

Years later Sandi met John, her future husband. When they began dating, he told Sandi that the one thing he remembered most about his childhood was his mom's grasshopper pie. What are the odds? Clearly these people were destined for matrimony. It was a green match, and Sandi's love life came full circle.

Grasshopper pie is light and buoyant. It gives you the cool, refreshing sensation you get from mint chip ice cream. Because of the shamrock color, you just can't take life too seriously while you're eating it.

{ *However, there are some things only a mom can do . . . like mend a broken heart.*

# Grasshopper Pie MAKES 1 (9-INCH) PIE

**CHOCOLATE WAFER CRUST**

1    (9-ounce) box chocolate wafers

¼    cup granulated sugar

4 or 5 tablespoons butter, melted

**FILLING**

28    large marshmallows

½    cup whole milk

1    cup heavy whipping cream, chilled

4 to 6 drops green food coloring

¼    cup green crème de menthe

3    tablespoons white crème de cacao

Grasshoppers

**To make the crust:** Preheat the oven to 350°F. In the bowl of a food processor, pulse the wafers until crushed. Add the sugar and pulse again. While the machine is on, add the melted butter, starting with 4 tablespoons and adding more only if needed, until a coarse meal forms. Press the mixture firmly and evenly in the bottom and up the sides of a 9-inch pie pan. Bake for 10 minutes to set. Remove from the oven and set aside to let cool.

**To make the filling:** Place the marshmallows and milk in a large saucepan over low heat. Stir constantly with a wooden spoon until melted. Pour the mixture into a small bowl and chill for 30 minutes to 1 hour, until cold.

In the bowl of a stand mixer fitted with the whisk attachment, whip the cream until stiff peaks form. Add the drops of food coloring until the cream is bright kelly green, like a shamrock. Use a spatula to fold in the marshmallow mixture until fully incorporated. Do not beat. Stir in the crème de menthe and crème de cacao. Pour the filling into the crust. Chill for at least 4 hours or up to overnight.

## SUGAR MOMMAS TIPS

*sugar mommas notes:* This is the perfect recipe for St. Patrick's Day, Christmas, birthdays, or any occasion that requires a "Cheer up."

If you're feeling ambitious, use Momma Reiner's Homemade Marshmallows (page 269) in your filling.

*sass it up:* Serve with whipped cream (see Annabelle's Whipped Cream Topping, page 71). Sprinkle on a topping to decorate your pie, such as crushed Andes mints, green candy canes, cookie crumbs, or chocolate shavings. For a more intense mint experience, you may want to drizzle some crème de menthe on top.

*old school:* Granny Helen used to put a metal bowl in the freezer until chilled, then whip the cream to stiff peaks in the bowl before folding in the marshmallow.

*carpool crunch:* Use a ready-made chocolate cookie crust in a pinch.

# savoie family *pies* and *pick-ups*

The Savoie family knows sugar. Charles Clarence Savoie Sr. ("Papa") and Ursula Prados Savoie ("Mimi") expanded the family sugar business when they acquired the Lula Sugar Factory in Belle Rose, Louisiana, in 1934. In a typical year, the factory will grind about 2.1 million tons of cane, producing an estimate 440 million pounds of raw sugar.

Family members have managed these companies for at least four generations. They approach the task pragmatically: "We all realize that there will be disagreements on how to run things, but once the dust settles, we walk away friends, and we never mix social with business." They never discount the value of "social," either. This is reflected by their many annual reunions and gatherings.

Charles Savoie Sr. was the patriarch of the family sugar business as well as of his large Louisiana brood. He was also Suzanne Tierney's loving grandfather. Mr. Savoie started a family tradition more than 50 years ago of bringing the entire family together for Easter weekend.

The 11 children and multitude of grandchildren would descend upon a resort. They feasted on fish on Friday, reveled in "adult night" on Saturday, and attended church services on Sunday. As the kids grew up, they participated in typical teenage shenanigans while the grown-ups were out celebrating Saturday evening. Now that they have all grown, their children are doing the same. Like Louisiana heat, some things are just predictable.

Suzanne has proudly attended "Easter Weekend" every year of her life. The entire clan stays connected to their sugar ancestry through this festive annual family reunion.

{
- Bev's Fraîche Fruit Pies
- Pecan Pick-Ups

# Bev's Fraîche Fruit Pies

*Submitted by Suzanne Tierney*
*From her aunt Beverly Savoie Hunley's recipe, Covington, Louisiana*

Suzanne's aunt Beverly ("Aunt Bev") grew up in the 1950s, the oldest of Charles and Ursula Savoie's 11 children, and she was very active in 4-H (Head, Heart, Hands, and Health). Typical of rural towns, Beverly learned many practical skills through the club. Some of the kids focused on raising animals or gardening. Beverly loved sewing and cooking, especially making desserts. Beverly won prizes on the local level, and she competed on the state level in the pie contest. All of her siblings remember sampling what seemed like endless pies while Beverly was *practicing*. It was during this time that Beverly mastered pie perfection.

In the 1970s, Beverly was called upon by her sister Charlene to supply fruit pies to her restaurant, the Dante Street Deli, in New Orleans. The strawberry and lemon varieties that follow were quite popular. Now a retired nurse and mother of four, Beverly is still well known for her pies.

> *All of her siblings remember sampling what seemed like endless pies while Beverly was* practicing.

# Fraîche Strawberry Pie MAKES 1 (9-INCH) PIE

1 single-crust pie shell from this chapter, or 1 ready-made 9-inch pie crust, prebaked and cooled completely

4 cups strawberries, cleaned and cut in half (divided)

¾ cup water

1 cup granulated sugar

3½ tablespoons cornstarch

1 teaspoon fresh lemon juice

3 or 4 drops red food coloring

1 batch Fraîche Whipped Cream Topping (recipe follows)

4-H clover

Line the baked crust with 3 cups of the strawberries. For a perkier presentation, stand the strawberries up (stem side down) and place them in concentric circles. Set aside.

In a large saucepan over medium heat, simmer the remaining 1 cup berries with the water for 4 to 5 minutes. Mash with a fork. In a separate bowl, mix the sugar and cornstarch, then add to the saucepan. Simmer until the mixture is thick and clear (not cloudy) and the sugar is completely dissolved, about 10 minutes. Stir in the lemon juice and food coloring. Remove from the heat and let cool for 5 minutes. Pour the glaze mixture over the berries in the crust (see Sugar Mommas Note). Chill for 1 hour, or until cool. Serve with the whipped cream topping.

*sugar mommas note:* When filling the pie, Momma Reiner likes to dab the glaze on, around, and in between the strawberries with a pastry brush. That way if the strawberries are naturally very sweet (as they are during peak season), the glaze enhances their flavor instead of overwhelming the fruit.

## Fraîche Whipped Cream Topping

1   cup whipping cream

1   tablespoon granulated sugar

1   teaspoon vanilla extract

¼   teaspoon unflavored gelatin (optional)

In the bowl of a stand mixer fitted with the whisk attachment, whip the cream on high speed until it begins to stiffen. Add the sugar, vanilla, and gelatin (if elected) and beat on high speed until soft peaks form. Aunt Bev says the whipped cream will keep better if you add the gelatin.

*notes* _____

_____

_____

_____

_____

# Lemon Pie MAKES 1 (9-INCH) PIE

¾ cup granulated sugar

2 tablespoons all-purpose flour

2 tablespoons cornstarch

¼ teaspoon salt

1¼ cups hot water

Juice and grated zest of 3 medium lemons (zest optional)

3 large eggs

1 tablespoon butter

1 single-crust pie shell from this chapter or 1 ready-made 9-inch pie crust, prebaked and cooled completely

1 batch Fraîche Whipped Cream Topping (page 101)

Red Rooster Cocktail

In a large glass or other microwave-safe bowl, whisk together the sugar, flour, cornstarch, and salt. Stir in the hot water. Cook in the microwave on high power for 2 minutes. Remove and stir until smooth. Return to the microwave and cook for 90 seconds. Remove and mix until smooth. Stir in the lemon juice and zest, if desired.

In a separate small bowl, whisk the eggs. To temper the eggs, pour about 1 cup of the hot lemon mixture into the bowl of eggs. Quickly whisk them together, then slowly blend the egg mixture back into the hot lemon filling, stirring constantly. Stir in the butter. Return the bowl to the microwave and cook for 90 seconds. Remove and stir. Repeat in 90-second intervals until the mixture is as thick as pudding. Pour the filling into the cooled crust. Refrigerate 1 hour, or until chilled. Serve with whipped cream topping.

*notes*

# Red Rooster Cocktail SERVES 12 TO 18

Enjoy your next family gathering New Orleans—style with a refreshing beverage. Aunt Bev recommends the Red Rooster—a frozen slush that is especially good as a cooling afternoon or evening cocktail.

1   (12-ounce) can frozen orange juice concentrate

1   (64-ounce) bottle cranberry juice cocktail

4   cups vodka

1 or 2 drops red food coloring (optional)

Mosquito swatter

Combine the ingredients together (adding the food coloring if desired) in a large bowl and stir. Pour into large plastic pitchers. Freeze to make a "slushy" drink, or chill and serve over ice. For the slushy, spoon the frozen mixture into cocktail glasses, stir to loosen a little, and serve with a small straw or stirrer.

# Pecan Pick-Ups

*Submitted by Beverly Savoie Hunley*
*From her mother Ursula ("Mimi") Prados Savoie's recipe, New Orleans, Louisiana*

When your family business is sugar, you're sure to have some great desserts. Beverly remembers making pecan tartlets for the first time. It was for a wedding party her mother, Ursula, was giving in honor of a cousin. Ursula asked Beverly, then a young bride, to make the tartlets. They came out perfect, and everyone at the party was so impressed that they were homemade. The mini tarts became a tradition, and decades later, Beverly is still expected to "do" Pecan Pick-Ups whenever there is a family soiree. These tartlets are perfect for a shindig because you can just pick them up and pop them in your mouth without having to put down your cocktail.

{ *These tartlets are perfect for a shindig because you can just pick them up and pop them in your mouth without having to put down your cocktail.*

# Pecan Pick-Ups MAKES 36 MINI TARTS

### CREAM CHEESE MINI CRUSTS

3 ounces cream cheese, at room temperature

½ cup (1 stick) butter, at room temperature

1 cup all-purpose flour

### FILLING

2 large eggs

1 cup packed light brown sugar

2 tablespoons butter, melted

1 teaspoon vanilla extract

⅛ teaspoon salt

1 cup chopped pecans

**To make the crusts:** Place the cream cheese and butter in the bowl of a stand mixer fitted with the paddle attachment and beat on medium speed until creamy, about 1 minute. Add the flour and mix until a soft dough forms. Lightly flour your hands and then form the dough into a ball. Cover and refrigerate in the bowl for at least 1 hour or up to overnight. When chilled, break off 1 teaspoonful of dough and form it into a small ball. Press it into the bottom of a miniature muffin pan and use your fingers to gently press the dough halfway up the sides of the mini muffin cup. Repeat with the remaining dough. Refrigerate the pans while you prepare the filling.

**To make the filling:** Preheat the oven to 325°F. In a large bowl, whisk the eggs slightly. Stir in the sugar and butter. Add the vanilla, salt, and pecans and mix until the pecans are evenly coated.

Fill the dough cups about two-thirds full. Bake for 25 to 30 minutes. Remove from the oven and let cool for 2 to 3 minutes only before carefully removing the tarts from the pans (see Sugar Mommas Notes). This will prevent them from crisping too much and breaking as you remove them. If this does happen, however, just put the pans back in the oven for a minute or two to soften them a bit. Serve the pick-ups immediately, or refrigerate them in an airtight container until ready to serve. The pick-ups may also be stored in a tightly covered container in the freezer for up to 2 weeks.

# SUGAR MOMMAS TIPS

_sugar mommas notes:_ If you are making the mini tarts ahead of time, we recommend popping them in the microwave for 10 to 15 seconds before serving, because they are just divine warm.

You may use a pointed knife edge to help loosen the shells from their molds, then turn the pan over on parchment paper and use a knife to gently tap the bottom. The pick-ups should pop right out.

_old school:_ Aunt Bev uses raw sugar from her family's mill in place of brown sugar.

# Lemon Starlets

*Submitted by Catherine Watson*
*From her mother-in-law Chester Watson's recipe, Jackson, Mississippi*

We learned of Catherine Watson as a woman who enjoyed her dessert while soaking in the bathtub. We felt she might be a long-lost cousin—a soul sister who appreciated sweets as much as we do.

Catherine received this recipe from her mother-in-law, Chester. Chester was like an executive chef—she was superb at telling other people what to do in the kitchen. However, she did not cook herself. When she tried a dessert she liked, she would ask for the recipe and deliver it to Catherine, saying, "I think you might like it." This was code for "Why don't you make it for us?" This is how the Lemon Starlets came to be.

Chester used to say that people do not eat sweets at a cocktail party. Never one to acquiesce, Catherine always has a sideboard full and, as she told us, *somebody* is eating them. One of her favorite desserts is these mini lemon tarts.

In Catherine's words, "I still like to stick in a few pick-ups for guests who don't want to totally abandon their figures!" Single ladies, take note—we're told that men love this dessert, and it will certainly drive you to pucker up.

These are tangy lemon tartlets with *zing* in a fragile shortbread mini cup. With the first bite, the shell crumbles while the lemon curd tantalizes your tongue. Although the crust is delicious, we think its sole purpose is to ensure that you don't look like a freak at parties licking the lemon filling off your index finger. (Once the guests depart, have at it.) The meringue topping that follows is an optional variation, but is well worth a taste.

> *"I love sugar so much, I named my dog Sugar so I could go outside and holler, 'Come here, Sugar!'"*
>
> —CATHERINE WATSON

# Lemon Starlets MAKES 36 MINI TARTS

## TART SHELLS

1    cup all-purpose flour

¼    cup granulated sugar

⅛    teaspoon salt

¼    cup (½ stick) butter, at room temperature

1    egg yolk (reserve the white for meringue topping, if desired)

¼    teaspoon almond extract

## FILLING

2    large eggs

2    egg yolks (reserve the whites for meringue topping, if desired)

½    cup (1 stick) butter

1    cup granulated sugar

Juice and grated zest of 2 large lemons

Cocktail party "to-do" list

**To make the tart shells:** Preheat the oven to 400°F. In a large bowl, whisk together the flour, sugar, and salt. Stir in the butter, then the egg yolk, and then the almond extract. Use your hands to shape the dough. Pinch off a piece, roll it into a ball about the diameter of a quarter, and press it into the bottom and halfway up the sides of a mini muffin cup. You want the dough to be thin, as it puffs when it cooks. Repeat with the remaining dough.

Bake for 8 to 10 minutes, until golden. Let cool for 2 to 3 minutes only before carefully removing the shells from the pans (see Sugar Mommas Notes). This will prevent them from crisping too much and breaking as you remove them. If this does happen, however, just put the pans back in the oven for a couple of minutes to soften the shells a bit. Let cool completely before filling. The shells may be stored in a tightly covered container in the freezer for up to 1 month.

**To make the filling:** Fill the bottom of a double boiler (see Sugar Mommas Notes) with 1 to 2 inches of water and bring to a rolling boil. Place the whole eggs and yolks in the top of the double boiler off the heat. Beat gently with a fork or whisk until the whites and yolks are thoroughly mixed. Place the top of the double boiler back in place over medium-low heat. Stir constantly, watching the eggs carefully so that they don't start to curdle (see Sugar Mommas Notes).

Add the butter, sugar, lemon juice, and zest. Cook over gently boiling water, stirring often with a wooden spoon, until the mixture is the consistency of mayonnaise. This takes 10 minutes or so, and you do need to let it sit for a minute or two without stirring or it won't thicken. You can see it thicken around the rim of the double boiler. Remove from the heat and let set for 5 minutes.

Pour the filling into a glass bowl and place a piece of plastic wrap across the surface (so a skin doesn't form) and refrigerate for at least 1 hour or up to overnight. Fill the tart shells with the filling and serve. The filling will keep in a covered container in the refrigerator if you dare (Momma Reiner would eat it within an hour) for up to 2 weeks. The shells can be frozen for uo to 1 month. Leftover assembled tartlets will keep, covered, in the refrigertator for a few days.

*notes*

*"If the recipe says, "Serve immediately," I'm afraid I will have to turn the page."*

—CATHERINE WATSON

## Sugar Mommas
## Meringue Topping

4    **egg whites (reserved from making the shells and filling)**

½    **cup granulated sugar**

½    **teaspoon vanilla extract**

Preheat the oven to 400°F. In the bowl of a stand mixer fitted with the whisk attachment, beat the egg whites on high speed until foamy, about 30 seconds. Reduce the speed to medium, slowly add the sugar and vanilla, and mix until the whites are glossy, about 1 minute. Place 36 lemon tartlets (or less, if you do not wish to top them all) on a baking sheet and spoon about 1 heaping teaspoon of meringue over the top of each. Bake for 4 to 5 minutes, until slightly browned.

*notes*

*sugar mommas notes:* You may use a pointed knife edge to help loosen the tart shells from their molds, then turn the pan over on parchment paper and use a knife to gently tap the bottom. The mini crusts should pop right out.

If you don't have a double boiler, you may use a metal bowl nestled in a pot of boiling water (the water should remain at least 2 inches below the bottom of the bowl).

If your eggs scramble a little in the double boiler, do not fret. Use a spatula to push the filling through a fine-mesh strainer before serving to remove any little bits of egg so that it has a smooth consistency.

*modern variation:* Use the leftover egg whites to make a meringue topping, or use whipped topping. Put the meringue or whipped topping on some, but not all, of the tartlets. That way you'll create a little diversity in your display.

*sass it up:* If you're using meringue or whipped topping, place a single red raspberry on top to add color. Drizzle Cardinal Sauce (page 53) on the dessert plate if you are preparing individual servings.

# Ooey-Gooey Butter Tarts

*Submitted by Helen Pisani*
*From her grandmother Margaret Mae Taylor's recipe, Jeanette's Creek, Ontario*

In the late nineteenth century, Margaret Taylor lived on a farm in Ontario. With potatoes, wheat, corn, and oats among their crops, the Taylors required a lot of help from local laborers. This meant a number of mouths to feed. Margaret's daughter Gladys was born in 1913, and when she was old enough, she helped her mother bake pies from sunup to sundown to feed the farmhands. There were no modern amenities like dishwashers and microwaves, so the job involved long hours and arduous work.

Gladys eventually had a daughter, Helen, and they lived in Jeanette's Creek across the field, "maybe 30 rows of potatoes," from Margaret's house until Helen was married. As a girl, Helen remembers seeing these freshly made pastries sitting on a platter in her grandmother's kitchen waiting to be eaten. She would sneak off with one, and sit on the back step secretly enjoying all that sweet dripping goo. Gladys would occasionally catch her and just laugh. How could she resist?

You can't begin to understand how otherworldly these tarts are until you taste them. Momma Jenna says these are the pièce de résistance. After putting her son to bed, she loves to snuggle on the couch with her cats, a cup of hot tea or tall glass of milk, and a plate full of butter tarts. Her husband snatches one at his own risk. Momma Reiner likens the tarts to sticky buns on steroids. The crust is light and flaky, filled with warm caramel goop. JoJo, our student carpool taste-tester, claims they taste like crème brûlée crossed with pecan pie.

{ *Momma Reiner likens the tarts to sticky buns on steroids.*

# Ooey-Gooey Butter Tarts MAKES 12 TO 14 TARTS

## TART SHELLS

2 cups all-purpose flour

1 teaspoon salt

½ cup (1 stick) butter, cold

¼ cup vegetable shortening

1 teaspoon distilled white vinegar

¼ cup minus 1 teaspoon ice-cold water

## FILLING

¾ cup packed light brown sugar

1 tablespoon butter, at room temperature

1 large egg

½ cup light corn syrup

2 tablespoons heavy whipping cream

1 teaspoon vanilla extract

⅛ teaspoon ground nutmeg

½ cup chopped pecans

½ cup raisins (optional)

Personal time to enjoy these tarts undisturbed

**To make the tart shells:** Place the flour, salt, butter, and vegetable shortening in the bowl of a food processor and pulse about 10 times, until the mixture resembles small peas. Place the vinegar in a measuring cup, then add the ice water until you reach ¼ cup total. Add the vinegar mixture to the processor by the spoonful while pulsing until the mixture holds together. If the dough mixture does not flake in your hands, add extra shortening (but not more than an additional ¼ cup) to achieve the proper flaky consistency. Carefully turn out the dough onto parchment paper and shape it into a ball. Wrap it in plastic wrap or parchment paper and chill for at least 1 hour or up to overnight.

Roll out the dough on a lightly floured work surface until it is about ¼ inch thick. Using a cup or small bowl as a stencil, cut twelve to fourteen 4-inch circles. Use a spatula to gently lift each circle, then press the dough into a standard muffin cup. Flute or crimp the edges. Place the muffin pan in the refrigerator to chill while you prepare the filling.

**To make the filling:** Preheat the oven to 425°F. Place the sugar and butter in the bowl of a stand mixer fitted with the paddle attachment and beat on medium speed until well combined. Mix in the egg and blend until creamy, about 1 minute. Add the corn syrup, cream, vanilla, and nutmeg, one at a time, and mix until all the brown sugar clumps have broken up and you have a smooth syrup. Use a wooden spoon or spatula to fold in the pecans, and raisins, if desired. Fill the tart shells three-quarters full. Bake for 9 to 13 minutes, until the filling is bubbling and the crust is light brown. Remove from the oven and let cool for 5 minutes, then remove from the pan and let cool completely.

{ *Momma Jenna leaves out the raisins and pecans and any other "foreign objects," so that nothing disrupts her pure, unadulterated goo experience. Her husband has also been notified that swiping the last butter tart is grounds for jewelry-bearing apologies.*

## SUGAR MOMMAS TIPS

*sugar mommas note:* These tarts freeze well and are delicious to eat partially frozen. Helen calls them Icy Cold Goo.

*carpool crunch:* Use French Picnic pre-made frozen pie pastry (organic flour, pure butter, no preservatives) for the crust in this recipe. It comes in the form of flat, round circles—no need to roll them out.

*old school:* These tart shells were originally made with lard instead of shortening.

CHAPTER

4

# better
## than nooky
## cookies

Children grow up eating a certain cookie. They want it in their lunch boxes, as an after-school treat, sent in a care package to camp, or packed in the car for a road trip. The cookie is more than the sum of its ingredients—it is a symbol of home.

The cookie operates in the present. You make it, bake it, and eat it straight from the oven. Honestly, who waits for a cookie to cool? Momma Reiner says, "I remember my mom removing the baking sheet from the oven, using a spatula to lift a cookie, and putting it on a paper towel. She'd hand it to me, and I would carefully break the piping hot cookie apart and slide it into my mouth. That technique must have been genetically transferred, because that is exactly what I do with my children. I pass them the paper towel with wholesome gooey goodness on top. Cookies just taste better straight out of the oven."

We made discoveries in this chapter. There were cookies in old recipe boxes that we had never heard of before, that had been forgotten and discarded. We came across Chocolate Cloud Cookies, Cakies, Sugar Cakes, Buffalo Cookies, and Boobie Cookies. Yes, you read that correctly. One of our favorite revelations was Kossuth Cakes. Perhaps they were an ancestral cousin to the Whoopie Pie? Who cares? We have Whoopie Pies, too (see Candy and Creative Confections, Chapter 6).

We also learned that sugar transcends religious labels. The recipes in this chapter have connections to the Quaker, Mormon, Christian, Catholic, and Jewish traditions. We can say for certain that cookies from every faith taste divine.

# Gran's Tea Cakes

*Submitted by Barbara Mashburn Mayo*
*From her grandmother-in-law Rosa Stokes Cloud's recipe, Canton, Mississippi*

This recipe for tea cakes was passed down from Rosa Stokes Cloud, reared on the Stokes Plantation in Canton, Mississippi. Rosa taught her daughter, Lee Cloud Mayo, who in turn instructed her daughter-in-law, Barbara Mayo, how to make this dainty cookie. As Barbara recalls, Lee (aka "Gran") was loved by all who knew her, but she was not well known for her culinary skills. Despite her lack of gastronomic excellence, Gran made the best darn tea cakes you've ever tasted.

Gran had three sons, so dough was always in the refrigerator ready to bake when the boys came home from school. The house retained a wonderful nutmeg aroma of freshly baked cookies when visitors came by. Now Barbara carries on the tradition of Southern hospitality by offering these cookies to her drop-in company.

When we first heard about tea cakes, we could not help but be intrigued. The name sounds so elegant and graceful. We loved the idea that this custom dates back at least three generations. We asked Mrs. Mayo, "When do you eat these?" She replied in a lovely drawl, "Well, honey, we eat tea cakes every day!"

These petite cookies smell so glorious that we wanted to leap into the oven. The second the timer buzzed, we made frothy cappuccinos, sat at the kitchen table, exhaled, and actually relaxed for 5 minutes. The Mayos are on to something!

{ *We asked Mrs. Mayo, "When do you eat these?" She replied in a lovely drawl, "Well, honey, we eat tea cakes every day!"*

# Gran's Tea Cakes MAKES ABOUT 6 DOZEN TEA CAKES

| | | | | |
|---|---|---|---|---|
| 5 | cups all-purpose flour | | 1 | cup vegetable shortening |
| 1 | teaspoon salt | | 2 | cups granulated sugar |
| 1 | teaspoon baking powder | | 2 | large eggs |
| 1 | teaspoon baking soda | | 1 | teaspoon vanilla extract |
| 1 | teaspoon ground nutmeg | | ¾ | cup whole milk |
| | | | | Door chime |

In a medium bowl, whisk together the flour, salt, baking powder, baking soda, and nutmeg. Set aside. Place the shortening and sugar in the bowl of a stand mixer fitted with the paddle attachment and beat on medium speed until creamy. Reduce the speed to low and add the eggs, one at a time. Add the vanilla. Add half the flour mixture and blend. Slowly incorporate the milk. Add the remaining flour mixture and blend until smooth. Cover tightly with plastic wrap. Chill in the refrigerator for at least 2 hours.

Preheat the oven to 350°F. Line baking sheets with parchment paper (or use nonstick cooking spray). Use a tablespoon to scoop the cookie dough, roll it into a ball, and place it on a baking sheet, leaving at least 1 inch between the cookies. Repeat with the remaining dough. Dip a fork into flour (to prevent sticking) and make a crisscross pattern on the top of each cookie by piercing it with the prongs. Bake the cookies for 10 minutes, or until the edges begin to brown. Remove from the oven. Cool for 1 minute, then transfer to a wire rack and let cool completely.

notes

## SUGAR MOMMAS TIPS

*sugar mommas notes:* We love that you make a huge bowl of dough to keep in the fridge. When the mood strikes you, scoop some out and bake it. As we made them, friends and neighbors kept coming over to take chunks of dough to bake at home. Every house in the neighborhood smelled of nutmeg.

We use a small ice-cream scoop (#50) to make uniform cookies. Don't forget to dip the scoop in flour and shake off the excess to prevent sticking, or use nonstick spray.

*sass it up:* Instead of a fork, use a cake-decorating comb or other patterned utensil to make designs on top of your tea cakes.

*old school:* The original recipe was made with lard instead of vegetable shortening.

# Boobie Cookies

*Submitted by Momma Jenna*
*From her grandmother Ann Pinto's recipe, Milford, Connecticut*

Like so many wonderful home bakers, Grandma churned out various and sundry treats every year for Christmas. Gram's cookie platters put the local bakery to shame. She approached her trays like antipasto—they needed to consist of a variety of shapes, colors, textures, and tastes. If you were a lucky recipient of Gram's holiday assortment, you could probably feed your family of six for a month, though you would start the new year with your belt loosened a couple of notches.

One of Gram's most endearing traits was that she made up fun names for her cookie inventions. One day while Gram was cooking, two grandkids came to visit and asked her if she had any "boobie cookies." Gram was perplexed. The name didn't ring a bell until she realized they were referring to the cookies with the pointy tip. Needless to say, everyone had a good laugh, and these cookies were forever after known in our family as Boobie Cookies.

{ *One day while Gram was cooking, two grandkids came to visit and asked her if she had any "boobie cookies."*

# Boobie Cookies MAKES 4½ DOZEN COOKIES

3 cups all-purpose flour

1 teaspoon baking soda

½ teaspoon salt

1 cup (2 sticks) butter, at room temperature

1 cup granulated sugar

½ cup packed light brown sugar

2 large eggs, slightly beaten

1 teaspoon vanilla extract

54 chocolate Hershey's Kisses, unwrapped

Giggles

Preheat the oven to 375°F. Line baking sheets with parchment paper (or use nonstick cooking spray). Eat a few extra Kisses so you are not tempted to touch the 54 you prepared for the cookies.

In a small bowl, whisk together the flour, baking soda, and salt. Set aside. Place the butter and sugars in the bowl of a stand mixer fitted with the paddle attachment and beat on medium speed until creamy. Reduce the speed to low and add the eggs, one at a time. Add the vanilla. Add the flour mixture, a little at a time, and blend until smooth. Transfer the bowl from the stand mixer to a work surface near the baking sheets and unwrapped candy.

Scoop 1 teaspoon of cookie dough and roll it into a ball. Place it in the palm of your hand and push a chocolate Kiss into the center. Use your thumb, index finger, and middle finger to gently pull the dough up around the chocolate candy so that it is completely enclosed. Place each dough-wrapped Kiss on a baking sheet, leaving at least 2 inches between each cookie.

Bake for 7 to 9 minutes, until the cookies are lightly golden. Remove from the oven and cool for 1 minute, then transfer to a wire rack to let cool completely.

_notes_

_sugar mommas notes:_ The first time you make the cookies, we suggest baking just one sheet to see how the cookies spread out in the oven. That will help you determine how much dough to use and how best to shape each cookie for the remainder of the batch.

Momma Reiner has made these cookies for her friends afflicted with breast cancer. They always elicit a smile. We think they are the perfect contribution to a breast cancer fundraising bake sale.

# Christa's Chocolate Chip—Pecan Cookies

***Submitted by Christa Miller***
*From her mother Bonnie Beatrice Trompeter's recipe, New York, New York*

Christa Miller understands our cookie obsession. In an attempt to instill good eating habits, she was encouraged to eat a healthy diet during the week by her super-model mother, Bonnie Beatrice Trompeter. There was a strict "no junk food" policy Monday through Friday. Weekly meals consisted of protein toast, grilled chicken, vegetables, salad, and Tab diet cola. Ahhh . . . remember the Tab?

On the weekends, the family traveled from the city to the countryside. Upon their arrival in Quogue, on Long Island, the first thing they did was stock up on "week-end food" at the market. The grocery basket was filled with the Kellogg's Fun Pak, which included small boxes of Cocoa Krispies, Apple Jacks, and Froot Loops. They also grabbed an Entenmann's crumb cake and maybe even a jelly doughnut from the local deli on the way home. Once the groceries were put away, the Friday night ritual included dinner at Sherman's Restaurant for fried chicken, soft squishy rolls, and salad coated with French dressing. Usually the end result was an excellent night of sleep.

Saturday was spent preparing for the guests destined to arrive for the weekly dinner party. In between the usual kid activities of bike riding, tennis, and ice-skating, Christa would bake various desserts, including banana cake and meringue cookies. Her favorite recipe was this one, for chocolate chip—pecan cookies.

Ever since those childhood weekends in the country, Christa has been on a personal quest for her sweet holy grail—the perfect chocolate chip cookie. Starting with a basic recipe from her mother's kitchen, she spent years crafting and refining her masterpiece. She has, on occasion, veered off in the wrong direction, including an attempt at the "healthy" chocolate chip cookie, made with wheat flour and flaxseed. Thank goodness she came to her senses and found her way back to the sugar side! After 30 years of experimenting, Christa has just recently declared that with *this* recipe, she has reached the pinnacle of cookie Zen.

Now when on hiatus from work, one of her favorite activities is baking these cookies for her husband and three children. After making a batch, Christa eats a few and sets the rest aside in a resealable plastic bag to freeze. She uses a Sharpie pen to mark the plastic bag with the "No" symbol—a big circle with a line going through it (think *Ghostbusters*) . . . touch at your own risk! Christa's husband, Bill, believes that "leftover chocolate chip cookies" is an oxymoron. He eats his allotment immediately. A flawless blend of salty and sweet, chewy and crunchy, these cookies are sure to please the most discerning palates.

{ *After 30 years of experimenting, Christa has just recently declared that with this recipe, she has reached the pinnacle of cookie Zen.*

# Christa's Chocolate Chip—Pecan Cookies MAKES 5 TO 6 DOZEN COOKIES

| | |
|---|---|
| 2 | cups all-purpose flour |
| 1 | teaspoon baking soda |
| 1 | heaping teaspoon salt |
| 1 | cup plus 2 tablespoons (2¼ sticks) butter, at room temperature |
| ½ | cup granulated sugar |
| ½ | cup packed light brown sugar |
| 2 | teaspoons vanilla extract (Christa uses Madagascar) |
| 2 | large eggs |
| 2 | cups semisweet chocolate chips |
| ½ | cup chopped pecans (shaken in a sieve to remove dust) |
| | Sea salt, for dusting (Christa uses Maldon) |
| | TGIF |

Preheat the oven to 375°F. In a medium bowl, whisk together the flour, baking soda, and salt. Set aside. Place the butter and sugars in the bowl of a stand mixer fitted with the paddle attachment and beat on medium speed until creamy. Add the vanilla. Reduce the speed to low and add the eggs, one at a time. Slowly add the flour mixture until just combined. Do not overwork the dough. Use a spatula or wooden spoon to fold in the chocolate chips and pecans.

Drop the dough by tablespoons onto ungreased baking sheets (or line baking sheets with parchment paper if you prefer), placing the cookies about 1 inch apart. Lightly sprinkle sea salt on top of each cookie. Bake for 10 to 12 minutes, until the edges begin to brown slightly. Remove from the oven. Cool for 1 minute, then transfer to a wire rack to let cool completely.

_notes_

*sugar mommas note:* Bill, her husband, likes his cookies a smidge under-cooked—baked for 8 minutes. Christa likes her cookies a tad well done—baked for 14 minutes. We like ours cooked through, yet soft and chewy so that the cookies still bend apart.

# Sugar Cakes

*Submitted by Sheila Becker*

*From her mother-in-law Grace Becker's recipe, Stoverstown, Pennsylvania*

Grace Becker, born April 7, 1914, introduced these delicious Sugar Cakes to her daughter-in-law, Sheila. The cookies originated in the Pennsylvania Dutch (an Americanized form of *Deutsch*, meaning "German") area of Stoverstown. Pennsylvania Dutch cooking is a specialty, and Sugar Cakes are part of the cooking heritage from those early German settlers. This recipe was handed down from family members who emigrated from Germany in the 1700s.

Grace was always in the kitchen cooking favorite recipes from her great-grandmother. Though Sugar Cakes look like cookies, they have a spongier, more cake-like texture and are not as sweet as typical sugar cookies. These were a summer favorite with lemonade and a winter favorite with hot chocolate. As each of the children went off to college, Sugar Cakes were mailed to them in waxed paper—lined shoe boxes to fulfill their cravings while away from home.

{ *This recipe was handed down from family members who immigrated from Germany in the 1700s.*

# Sugar Cakes MAKES ABOUT 6 DOZEN COOKIES

| | |
|---|---|
| 4 cups all-purpose flour | 3 large eggs |
| 1 teaspoon baking powder | 1 cup buttermilk |
| ½ cup (1 stick) butter, at room temperature | 1 teaspoon baking soda |
| ½ cup vegetable shortening | ¼ cup hot water |
| 2 cups granulated sugar, plus more for topping | 1 tablespoon vanilla extract |
| | Horse and carriage |

Preheat the oven to 375°F. Line baking sheets with parchment paper (or use nonstick cooking spray). In a medium bowl, whisk together the flour and baking powder. Set aside. Place the butter, shortening, and sugar in the bowl of a stand mixer fitted with the paddle attachment and beat on medium speed until creamy. Reduce the speed to low and add the eggs, one at a time. Add half the flour mixture and blend. Slowly incorporate the buttermilk. Add the remaining flour mixture and blend until smooth. Dissolve the baking soda in the hot water, stirring for 20 to 30 seconds, until the water is clear and no longer cloudy. Slowly blend into the mixture. Add the vanilla and beat until just combined.

The prepared dough should be baked immediately. Place any remaining dough in the refrigerator between batches to keep it chilled. Drop the dough by tablespoons onto the baking sheets s, placing the cookies about 1 inch apart. Sprinkle a generous amount of sugar on top of each, and gently press the sugar into the dough.

Bake for 10 to 11 minutes, until the edges begin to brown slightly. Remove from the oven and cool for 1 minute. Transfer to a wire rack to let cool completely.

*sass it up:* For a dramatic look, use large sparkling sugar in multicolored confetti, which can be found at specialty stores. We like India Tree sugar crystals. They make these cookies pop!

*notes*

# Candy Cane Cookies

*Submitted by Cyndy Frederick-Ufkes*
*From her grandmother Margretta Tays Riley's recipe, Lincoln, Nebraska*

In the late 1940s and early 1950s, Joan and her mother, Margretta Tays Riley, began the tradition of making candy cane—shaped cookies during the Christmas season. Joan brought them to school for her classmates and shared them with neighbors. Everyone got a kick out of the shape, and the treats were very popular. Joan carried on this tradition with her daughters, Cyndy and Deb.

Cyndy recalls that every December, her mother would make the dough and then let Cyndy and Deb dye half of it red. When the dough was chilled, the sisters would each be allowed to roll out her own "snakes" of red and white dough and twist them into candy cane shapes. Some would end up plump, and others wiry. The girls made batches for their own private stash at the beginning of December. In mid-December they would make more to share with friends, teachers, and neighbors. The cookies were also an essential dish at every family Christmas gathering, served on a red candy cane—shaped tray.

The cookies are the perfect treat to make with young children, because they can take part in the process without the added mess of frosting and sprinkles. The dough can easily be varied in color and shape to fit any theme. Although these were solely "special Christmas cookies" for Cyndy and Deb, now these women make the cookies with their children throughout the year.

> { *The cookies are the perfect treat to make with young children, because they can take part in the process without the added mess of frosting and sprinkles.*

# Candy Cane Cookies MAKES ABOUT 2 DOZEN COOKIES

| | |
|---|---|
| 2 cups all-purpose flour | 1 large egg |
| 1½ teaspoons baking powder | 1 tablespoon whole milk |
| ¼ teaspoon salt | 1 teaspoon vanilla extract |
| 6 tablespoons (¾ stick) butter, slightly chilled | 1 teaspoon peppermint or almond extract |
| ⅓ cup vegetable shortening | 2 teaspoons red food coloring (or more for desired color) |
| ¾ cup granulated sugar | List for Santa |

In a small bowl, whisk together the flour, baking powder, and salt. Set aside. Place the butter, shortening, and sugar in the bowl of a stand mixer fitted with the paddle attachment and beat on medium speed until creamy. Reduce the speed to low and add the egg and milk. Add the vanilla and peppermint (or almond) extracts and blend well. Slowly add the flour mixture and blend until smooth.

Remove half of the dough, form it into a ball, and cover tightly with plastic wrap. Add the red food coloring to the remaining dough and mix well until the desired color is reached. Form the red dough into a ball, cover tightly with plastic wrap, and refrigerate both balls of dough for at least 3 hours. For best results, place the dough in the freezer for 30 minutes prior to shaping the cookies. (The dough may be frozen for up to 1 month if wrapped tightly in plastic and then placed inside a resealable plastic freezer bag.)

Remove the dough from the freezer, cut each ball into thirds, and work with one-third at a time, leaving the rest in the freezer until ready to use.

Preheat the oven to 375°F. Line baking sheets with parchment paper (do not use nonstick cooking spray). Scoop 1 tablespoon of dough in each color and roll them into balls. Then roll out each ball into "snakes" about 7 inches long. Lay the "snakes" side by side, twist them around each other, and then bend them to form a candy cane shape. Slightly pinch each end of the candy cane to secure them. Use a spatula to transfer the cookie to a baking sheet. Repeat with the remaining dough, leaving at least 1 inch between cookies.

Bake for 8 to 9 minutes, until the dough looks dry but not brown. Remove from the oven and cool for 1 minute, then transfer to a wire rack to let cool completely.

_notes_

_**sugar mommas notes:**_ Let small children roll the dough into balls and snakes. Then Mom can come along and twist the snakes into candy cane shapes. As the kids get older, they can make the shapes.

If the peppermint flavor is too strong, use half the suggested amount, or use ½ teaspoon only in the red dough.

_**modern variation:**_ This is a terrific cookie base. Experiment with flavor, shapes, and color. Add a little pink or red food coloring to make hearts for Valentine's Day, or go red, white, and blue for the Fourth of July.

# Buffalo Chip Cookies

*Submitted by Irene Mangum*
*From Dorothy Cassidy Gayden's recipe, East Feliciana Parish, Louisiana*

Irene remembers her mother, Dorothy Cassidy Gayden, making these cookies when she was growing up in the 1940s and '50s on the Sunnyslope Plantation in East Feliciana Parish, Louisiana. Irene always assumed that the recipe originated in Texas because "All we've got here is alligators and snakes. We don't have buffalo in Louisiana!"

Whenever Irene made these cookies as an adult, people asked for the recipe, which she was glad to pass along. Irene claims that she was usually talking so fast, she forgot to add one instruction: "Mix by hand." Irene hates to admit that she forgot that vital instruction on more than one occasion, and that, perhaps, after a few incidents, all her friends threw the recipe away.

Her friend Zeita Parker couldn't wait to go home and make Irene's Buffalo Chip Cookies for her children. She wanted any excuse to use the brand-new stand mixer (the latest model) her mother-in-law had given her as a gift. Back in the late 1960s, it was like the latest model iPhone, but for the kitchen. Irene was kind enough to share her recipe. Zeita proceeded to make the cookies as instructed, adding all the ingredients to the bowl of her fancy kitchen appliance. The dough was so dense and chunky that the mixer jumped right off the counter like a scene from *The Twilight Zone*. It was whirling around on the floor possessed, throwing cookie dough into every corner of the kitchen! Even though the mixing bowl broke, the incident was so funny that it has provided years of intense, tear-inducing belly laughs.

We will guide you safely through this recipe, but trust us when we tell you it's time to *mix by hand*.

{ *The dough was so dense and chunky that the mixer jumped right off the counter like a scene from* The Twilight Zone.

# Buffalo Chip Cookies MAKES ABOUT 3 DOZEN LARGE COOKIES

4   cups all-purpose flour

2   teaspoons baking powder

2   teaspoons baking soda

1   cup (2 sticks) butter, at room temperature (Irene uses Land O'Lakes)

1   cup vegetable shortening

1   (16-ounce) box light brown sugar

2   cups granulated sugar

4   large eggs

2   teaspoons vanilla extract

2   cups old-fashioned rolled oats (not instant)

2   cups cornflakes

1   (12-ounce) package semisweet chocolate chips

1   cup chopped pecans (optional)

    Buffalo

Preheat the oven to 350°F. Line baking sheets with parchment paper (do not use nonstick cooking spray).

In a large bowl, whisk together the flour, baking powder, and baking soda. Set aside. Place the butter, shortening, and sugars in the bowl of a stand mixer fitted with the paddle attachment and beat on medium speed until creamy. Reduce the speed to low and add the eggs, one at a time. Add the vanilla. Add the flour mixture a little at a time, and blend until smooth. Remove the bowl from the stand. **Mix by hand** from this point forward. Use a spatula or wooden spoon to fold in the oats, cornflakes, chocolate chips, and pecans, if desired.

These cookies are *gigantic*. Use a tablespoon to drop 2 heaping spoonfuls of dough onto the baking sheet for each cookie, placing the cookies about 2 inches apart. Bake for 15 minutes, or until the cookies are lightly golden. Remove from the oven and cool for 5 minutes. Transfer to a wire rack to let cool completely.

*notes* _____

_____

_____

_____

_____

_____

_____

_____

_____

_____

_____

_____

_____

_____

_____

_____

_____

_____

## SUGAR MOMMAS TIPS

*sugar mommas nifty gadget:* Use Wilton's large cookie scoop to get that big ol' cookie size!

*sass it up:* Try different add-ins according to your preferences. Remove inclusions you don't like and toss in raisins, dried cranberries, coconut flakes, walnuts, butterscotch chips, peanut butter chips, or vanilla chips instead.

# Cracked Sugar Cookies

*Submitted by Kelly Allen Welsh*
*From Ruth Elaine Allen's recipe, Sac City, Iowa*

Ruthie grew up during the Depression on a farm in Sac City, Iowa. Tragedy took her father and brother at a very young age, so the three remaining members of the family pitched in to survive. Although it was rare for women to work during that time, her mother, Dessie Bell "Dott" Rhodes Brown, was lucky to get a job with the county. Ruthie's brother, 12-year-old Willie, delivered milk before school. That left Ruthie to manage the cooking at a very young age.

Through perseverance, Ruthie was the first person in her family to graduate from college, where she earned a teaching degree. She taught in Fort Dodge, Iowa, before deciding on a whim to travel to United Airlines headquarters to interview as a flight attendant. In those days, being a "stewardess" was a very glamorous job. Ruthie was hired even though she had never been close to an airplane. She served United for two years before she married and started a family.

> *"She looked like Eva Gabor in the '60s . . . big blond beehive."*

Ruthie's daughter, Kelly, idolized her mother and loved her for all the sacrifices she made and the strength she exhibited throughout her life. She is reminded of her mother every time she bites into a Cracked Sugar Cookie. "She looked like Eva Gabor in the '60s . . . big blond beehive. [She] had a deep love for home and family (probably because hers was torn apart by tragedy). Feeding the family was very important to my mother. I have fond memories of baking and cooking with my mom at a very young age. She touched everyone she met, from the lady behind the counter at the dry cleaners to the checkout gals from Dahl's grocery store to the gas station attendants (whom she always tipped because she felt she should share some of her good fortune in life)."

Kelly emulated Ruthie as a baker, as a mother, and as a flight attendant for American Airlines for 24 years. She loved to eat these cookies as a child, and she still enjoys them, rolled in sugar and baked to a crisp with cracks running through them. Kelly has carried on the tradition with her sons, and now she shares the recipe with you.

# Cracked Sugar Cookies MAKES ABOUT 6 DOZEN COOKIES

2¼ cups all-purpose flour

1 teaspoon baking soda

⅛ teaspoon salt

½ cup (1 stick) butter

½ cup margarine

2 cups granulated sugar, plus ½ cup more for rolling

3 egg yolks

1 teaspoon cream of tartar

½ teaspoon vanilla extract

½ teaspoon fresh lemon juice

Wings

In a large bowl, whisk together the flour, baking soda, and salt. Set aside. Place the butter, margarine, and 2 cups sugar in the bowl of a stand mixer fitted with the paddle attachment and beat on medium speed until creamy. Reduce the speed to low and add the egg yolks, one at a time. Add the cream of tartar, vanilla, and lemon juice and blend well. Add the flour mixture, a little at a time, and blend until smooth. Form the dough into a ball and cover tightly with plastic wrap. Chill in the refrigerator for at least 30 minutes.

Preheat the oven to 325°F. Line baking sheets with parchment paper (or use nonstick cooking spray). Place the remaining ½ cup of sugar in a small bowl and set aside. Remove the dough from the refrigerator and scoop a teaspoon of dough about the size of a quarter into the palm of your hand. Roll the dough into a ball. Roll the ball in the sugar and place it on a baking sheet. Repeat with the remaining dough, leaving 2 inches between cookies.

Bake for 11 to 13 minutes, until the cookies begin to brown on the edges. These cookies will look flat with cracks running through them. Remove from the oven and cool for 2 to 3 minutes. Transfer to a wire rack to let cool completely.

*sass it up:* Use large sparkling sugar in multicolored confetti, which can be found at specialty stores (we prefer India Tree sugar crystals).

*notes*

# After-School Oatmeal Cookies

*Submitted by Moira Hoyne Conlon*
*From school principal Stan Kerr's recipe, Montecito, California*

For Moira, the crisp autumn air of northern California in the early 1970s carried the sound of Neil Diamond records and the smell of oatmeal cookies. Her parents occasionally called on their friend Stan Kerr, the principal at Montecito Union Elementary School, to babysit Moira and her seven siblings. Who better to supervise the kids on a Saturday night? Moira remembers "Sweet Caroline" playing in the background while the kids baked oatmeal cookies in their olive green kitchen. Principal Kerr had figured out a way to teach math without protest.

We were amused that Principal Kerr's recipe was imprecise. Apparently, the principal lacked specificity and eyeballed his measurements, adding a pinch of this or a shake of that where necessary. If the kids were well behaved, he rewarded them by letting them put two cookies together with a dab of chocolate in the middle. Who said bribery wasn't an effective babysitting tool? In the Hoyne family, being sent to the principal had its perks.

> { *Moira remembers "Sweet Caroline" playing in the background while the kids baked oatmeal cookies in their olive green kitchen.*

# After-School Oatmeal Cookies MAKES ABOUT 6 DOZEN COOKIES

3   cups all-purpose flour

2   teaspoons salt

2   teaspoons baking soda

2   cups (4 sticks) butter, at room temperature

2   cups granulated sugar

2   cups packed light brown sugar

2   large eggs, well beaten

⅓   cup water

2   teaspoons vanilla extract

5   cups old-fashioned rolled oats (not instant)

Neil Diamond record

Preheat the oven to 350°F. In a medium bowl, whisk together the flour, salt, and baking soda. Set aside. Place the butter and sugars in the bowl of a stand mixer fitted with the paddle attachment and beat on medium speed until creamy. Reduce the speed to low and add the eggs, one at a time. Add the water and vanilla. Add the flour mixture, a little at a time, and blend until smooth. Use a spatula or wooden spoon to fold in the oats. Drop tablespoonfuls of dough onto ungreased baking sheets (or line baking sheets with parchment paper if you prefer), placing the cookies about 1 inch apart. Bake for 8 to 10 minutes, until the cookies are slightly brown. Remove from the oven and cool for 2 minutes. Transfer to a wire rack to let cool completely.

*notes*

# Princess Cutout Cookies

*Submitted by Kathy Grocott*
*From her mother Patricia Ann Lüetkehöelter's recipe, St. Paul, Minnesota*

Kathy and her sister celebrated every Halloween, Christmas, Valentine's Day, and Easter by making cutout cookies. "Mom, whenareyoumakingcutoutcookies?Canwe docutoutcookies? Thesewouldbegreatdecorationsforthecutoutcookies!" The siblings spent all year acquiring embellishments for their cookies. When the girls were old enough to be unsupervised, their mom would walk away and leave them around the kitchen table to their creativity and a giant mess.

Through consistent prodding and some persuasive begging, the little ladies would convince their mother to buy silver dragées. Kathy's mom would remind them that the tiny silver balls were to be used sparingly and not eaten. The girls each made a cookie completely covered with dragées—not a bit of frosting showing through. They thought it was hilarious and would holler out from the kitchen, "Look at the cookies we made especially for you, Mom!"

{ *Mom, whenareyoumakingcutoutcookies?Canwedocutoutcookies? Thesewouldbegreatdecorationsforthecutoutcookies!*

Unbeknownst to Kathy, while the girls thoroughly entertained themselves in the kitchen, their parents eavesdropped from the living room. They overheard their daughters giggling, chatting about their cookie-decorating genius, and whispering their secrets around the kitchen table. It's a wonder kids are shocked when their parents know everything.

Kathy is nostalgic every time she pulls out the baking instructions. In her own words, "The page is like an ancient Dead Sea Scroll encrusted with years of butter and sugar and, I'm sure, little hand spills that make it no longer just a piece of paper."

These are the best sugar cookies we have tasted! These treats remain soft and delicious when baked and do not get hard and crunchy like other sugar cookies. Just the thought of them evokes little girls dressed up in their princess costumes having a tea party and decorating cookies. Dust off your ballerina tutu and go to town!

# Princess Cutout Cookies MAKES ABOUT 4 DOZEN COOKIES

2½ cups all-purpose flour

1 teaspoon baking powder

1 teaspoon salt

½ cup (1 stick) butter, at room temperature

¼ cup vegetable shortening

1 cup granulated sugar

2 large eggs

1 teaspoon vanilla extract

1 batch Princess Cutout Cookie Frosting (recipe follows)

Sprinkles or other decorations

Tiara

In a small bowl, whisk together the flour, baking powder, and salt. Set aside. Place the butter, shortening, and sugar in the bowl of a stand mixer fitted with the paddle attachment and beat on medium speed until creamy. Reduce the speed to low and add the eggs, one at a time. Add the vanilla. Add the flour mixture, a little at a time, and blend until smooth. Form the dough into a ball and cover tightly with plastic wrap. Chill in the refrigerator for at least 1 hour.

Preheat the oven to 400°F. Remove the dough from the refrigerator and place it on a lightly floured work surface. Roll out to about a ⅛-inch thickness. Cut with a cookie cutter dusted with flour to prevent sticking. Use a spatula to transfer the cookies to ungreased baking sheets (or line baking sheets with parchment paper if you prefer). Bake for 6 to 7 minutes, until the cookies set. Remove from the oven and cool for 1 minute. Transfer to a wire rack to let cool completely. Frost and decorate with sprinkles.

*sugar mommas note:* When baking, do not wait for the cookies to brown or they will be overdone.

*modern variation:* Silver dragées are now illegal in many states. Get a similar look by using Wilton Pearlized Sprinkles.

## Princess Cutout Cookie Frosting

| 2 | cups confectioners' sugar |
|---|---|
| ¼ | cup whole milk, plus more as needed |
| ¼ | teaspoon vanilla or almond extract |
| | Food coloring (optional) |

Place the confectioners' sugar in a large bowl. Slowly whisk in the milk until the frosting reaches your desired consistency (we like it relatively thick). Add the extract and mix well. If you want colored frosting, add food coloring 1 drop at a time to get your preferred color.

We separate the frosting into three bowls and use different food coloring in each to make these cookies more festive. We also use a small pastry brush to glaze the cookies. Let the first layer dry, and then add another for stronger color.

*notes* _____

_____

_____

_____

_____

_____

# slice 'n' bake *gift* giving!

*Think of how hip you'll be when you drop off a log of homemade dough wrapped in pretty paper, tied with bows and a cute card for any occasion—teacher appreciation, thinking of you, happy birthday, sorry you had a crappy day, hostess gift, bummer your kid isn't sleeping through the night, pep up, or congratulations!*

*Prepare the dough logs as instructed, wrap them in plastic wrap, and place them in the refrigerator while you prepare the outer wrapping. Place a piece of decorative tissue paper facedown on a flat surface. (The design side of the tissue paper should be against the work surface.) Next, place a piece of parchment paper on top of the tissue paper. Remove the dough from the refrigerator and place the plastic-wrapped cookie log on top of the parchment paper. Starting at one end, roll the log and papers away from you until it looks like a big Tootsie Roll. Use a brightly colored ribbon to tie the overhang on each end. Decorate a small index card (or use scrapbooking paper to create one) with the baking instructions. Punch a hole in the corner of the card and attach it to the log with ribbon.*

*For sugar cookies (such as Princess Cutout Cookies), attach a cookie cutter or fancy sugar crystals for a special added touch. Place the wrapped dough inside a freezer-safe resealable plastic bag and freeze until you are ready to give it as a gift. The dough may be frozen for up to one month. To transport the cookie logs, place the bags in an insulated bag or cooler with a cold pack until you reach your destination. For a video demonstration, log on to www.SugarSugarRecipes.com.*

# Brown Sugar Slice 'n' Bakes

*Submitted by Sally Snow Halff Scully*
*From Alma Murphy Halff's recipe, Los Angeles, California*

Alma Murphy, born in the late 1880s, was a bohemian free spirit. Raised in New York, she had theatrical aspirations and became an actress with the David Belasco Theatre. (David Belasco is best known for writing *Madame Butterfly* for the stage, which was later adapted by Giacomo Puccini for opera.) Alma toured the United States with the Belasco theater troupe until she met and married Abraham Halff.

Throughout her marriage, Alma continued to dabble in acting and had her last child, John, in 1930 at age 42. Shortly thereafter, Alma's husband passed away, leaving her to raise four children. At the start of World War II, Alma's independent spirit led her to work for the defense industry at an aircraft factory. It comes as no surprise that Alma was at the forefront of the women's movement.

Throughout her escapades Alma loved to cook, and her gregarious nature was well suited to throwing parties. She taught her three daughters to cook, and entertaining became a family affair. This tradition continued during the holidays. The family came together to make Alma's cookies, which were then handed out as Christmas gifts to her vast circle of friends.

In the 1950s, Sally Snow married John Halff (Alma's youngest child), and as she tells us, "I married into a family of fabulous cooks. It was sink or swim; there was almost a moral responsibility to cook." Sally was quickly drawn into the Christmas cookie production.

Creating the cookies was a long and laborious process. Preparation started in October, when fresh nuts came into the markets in bulk for the holidays. Weeks were spent cracking, shelling, and chopping them. A sharp eye was needed for finding pretty cookie tins at a good price, as well as butter at an equally good price. Then Alma made the dough and stored it in the refrigerator until the time came to bake the cookies. Packaging the cookies was truly a spectacle. Each tin was carefully assembled and finished with crisp white doilies and bows. Presentation of the gift was satisfying to both the giver and the recipient.

In vintage-speak we would have called these icebox cookies. Because the Sugar Mommas are retro chic, we call them Brown Sugar Slice 'n' Bakes. The beauty of these cookies is that you can prepare them in advance. Make the cookie log on a weekend and freeze it. Then whip it out any day of the week. Slice off a few cookies to bake and eat while watching your favorite television show; or make an entire batch and invite some gal pals over for coffee. These cookies would also be perfect to serve at a planning committee meeting, wrapping party, or office brainstorming session.

{ *I married into a family of fabulous cooks. It was sink or swim; there was almost a moral responsibility to cook.*

# Brown Sugar
# Slice 'n' Bakes MAKES ABOUT 6 DOZEN COOKIES

5½ cups all-purpose flour

1 teaspoon baking soda

1 teaspoon salt

2 cups (4 sticks) butter, at room temperature

1½ cups granulated sugar

1 cup packed light brown sugar

2 large eggs

1 teaspoon vanilla extract

2 cups chopped pecans or walnuts (optional)

*Madame Butterfly*

In a large bowl, whisk together the flour, baking soda, and salt. Set aside. Place the butter and sugars in the bowl of a stand mixer fitted with the paddle attachment and beat on medium speed until creamy. Reduce the speed to low and add the eggs, one at a time. Add the vanilla. Add the flour mixture, a little at a time, and blend until smooth. Use a spatula or wooden spoon to fold in the nuts. Form the dough into a ball and cut it in half. Cover one half tightly in plastic wrap and chill in the refrigerator until you are ready to use it.

Place the remaining dough on a lightly floured work surface. Place two hands in the center of the dough and form it into a log, rolling back and forth and gently pushing from the center out toward the edges. Dust a piece of parchment paper lightly with flour and then place it over the dough log. If available, use a bamboo sushi mat or cloth on top of the parchment paper. Use your hands to shape the log, rolling back and forth, until it is about 6 inches long and 3 inches in diameter. Wrap the log in plastic wrap, making sure to cover the ends, and place it in a resealable plastic bag. Repeat with the other dough round. Chill the dough logs for at least 4 hours. (The dough may be frozen for up to 1 month.)

Preheat the oven to 350°F. Line baking sheets with parchment paper (or use nonstick cooking spray). Place the dough logs on a lightly floured cutting board or work surface. Cut them into ¼-inch-thick slices and place the slices on the prepared baking sheets, leaving at least 1 inch between cookies. Bake for 12 to 15 minutes, until the cookies are a medium brown color. If you like your cookies on the crispy side, you may want to cook them a minute longer, but watch carefully, as they go from crisp to burned quickly. Remove from the oven and cool for 1 minute. Transfer to a wire rack to let cool completely.

_notes_

_**Sugar mommas note:**_ In lieu of mixing the nuts into the cookie dough, we prefer to sprinkle a few nuts on top of the cookies once they have been sliced but before they have been baked. That way, we have the option to go bare or nutty.

# Four-Generation Ruggies

*Submitted by Hillary Siegal*
*From her great-grandmother Jenny Harris's recipe, Bronx, New York*

When someone says "Jewish pastry," the first thing that comes to mind is rugelach. Referred to as rugulach, rugalach, ruggalach, rogelach, rugalah, or rugala—no matter how you say or spell it, these treats are delicious. What are rugelach? In short, they are rolled cookies typically filled with jam, dried fruit, and nuts. There are several variations of rugelach, including different pastry dough recipes (with cream cheese or sour cream) and an endless possibility of fillings. *Rugelach* literally means "little twists" in Yiddish.

Hillary's great-grandmother Jenny Harris created a recipe for rugelach around 1935. When her daughter Eva (Hillary's grandmother) was a teenager, they became a family favorite. As Eva became an adult, Jenny brought the rugelach by train from the Bronx to the Lower East Side of Manhattan. Over the years, Eva carried them in shopping bags to Hillary's mother's house on Long Island. Trying to put her own twist on the recipe, Grandma Eva changed it ever so slightly by adding extra sour cream to the dough.

Hillary's mother, Sybil, also used this recipe, making some subtle alterations of her own. She created additional flavors, including raspberry with chocolate chips, and made them bite-size. These mini cookies are now affectionately called "Ruggies."

Sybil began bringing Ruggies to meetings, baby showers, dinner parties, and school bake sales. Some of Hillary's fondest memories growing up were of making rugelach in the kitchen with her mother. When she moved to the West Coast after college, it wasn't long before Hillary started having withdrawals from her mother's authentic New York Ruggies. Sybil would ship them in shoe box—size Tupperware containers. When they arrived, Hillary put the Ruggies into the freezer, as she loved to eat them cold. They didn't last long.

Now Hillary makes Ruggies for her children. Following in the ancestral footprints of strong-minded women, she has changed the recipe ever so slightly. Hillary created hazelnut-chocolate Ruggies and updated the family cinnamon-sugar recipe. After four generations, we present the lightest, crispiest, and most delicious version yet.

Here is Hillary's explanation of Ruggies in her own words:

"The Dough: This dough does not have cream cheese, only sour cream. Why leave out the cream cheese? The omission was either because my great-grandparents were too poor for the extra ingredient, or perhaps because my great-grandmother was onto something. The dough made with just the sour cream generates a pastry that is so flavorful and light, it melts in your mouth. When making the dough, work quickly. It is much easier working with dough that is cold and firm.

"The Filling: The process in creating rugelach is very social and collaborative. As children, making rugelach was the Jewish equivalent of creating your own personal pan pizza. The first layer was the jam: apricot, pineapple, raspberry, or strawberry. Next, we sprinkled on the toppings: chopped walnuts, raisins, chocolate chips, cinnamon, or sugar. It was a creative adventure that always proved to be a delicious success."

Hillary's most popular Ruggies flavor is hazelnut chocolate. This modern interpretation combines rich Nutella spread with milk chocolate and white chocolate chips. Even if you think you wouldn't like Rugelach, this version, which is like a tiny chocolate croissant, will win you over. It's always fun to experiment with new ingredients. Perhaps the recipe can be passed down through new generations with your own unique twist.

{ Rugelach *literally means "little twists" in Yiddish.*

# Four-Generation Ruggies MAKES 64 RUGELACH

2 cups all-purpose flour, plus more for dusting

½ cup granulated sugar

½ teaspoon salt

¾ cup sour cream

1 cup (2 sticks) butter, cold (cut into 1-tablespoon slices)

Filling for 64 Ruggies (recipes follow; see Sugar Mommas Note)

Egg whites, lightly beaten, for brushing the tops

Cinnamon sugar, for sprinkling the tops

Family tree

**Day 1:** In the bowl of a food processor, place the flour, sugar, salt, sour cream, and butter. Pulse 25 to 30 times, until the mixture resembles coarse meal. Do not overprocess—you should see pea-size chunks of butter in the dough.

Carefully turn out the dough onto parchment paper and form it into a ball. Cut it into quarters. Cover the dough segments tightly in plastic wrap and place in a resealable plastic freezer bag. Chill in the refrigerator overnight.

**Day 2:** Place the dough in the freezer for 30 minutes. When ready, remove one segment of the dough from the freezer and place it on a heavily floured work surface. Dust your rolling pin generously with flour. Divide the dough quarter in half. Rewrap the remaining portion and return it to the freezer for later. Roll out to an 8- to 9-inch circle about ⅛ inch thick.

Spread the prepared filling over the dough and cut it as instructed in the recipes that follow. Starting at the tops of the wedges, roll each slice of dough toward the pointed tip, like you would a crescent roll. As you roll, tuck the outside edges in toward the center. Repeat until all the cookies are rolled. Line a baking sheet with parchment paper. Place the Ruggies on the baking sheet, about 1 inch apart. These cookies do not rise or spread. Place the baking sheet in the freezer for 30 minutes, or until the Ruggies are firm.

Preheat the oven to 350°F. Remove the Ruggies from the freezer. Dip a pastry brush into the egg whites and lightly brush each cookie. Sprinkle cinnamon sugar on top of the cookies. Place the cookies into the oven while they are cold. Bake for 20 to 22 minutes, until golden. Remove from the oven and cool for 1 minute. Transfer to a wire rack to let cool completely.

*sugar mommas note:* Each filling recipe is for one one-eighth segment of the dough (8 Ruggies). If you choose to use the same filling for more of your Ruggies, you will need to multiply accordingly.

*carpool crunch:* You can store un-baked Ruggies in a sealed container in the freezer for up to 1 week. They can be baked directly from the freezer according to the instructions. Once the Ruggies are baked and cooled, they can be sealed in an airtight container and frozen up to 1 month.

*old school:* Hillary's relatives used Smucker's apricot-pineapple preserves in the traditional filling. Hillary uses Sarabeth's Kitchen Chunky Apple preserves in her traditional filling.

# Traditional Ruggie Filling
**FILLS 8 RUGGIES**

- 1 tablespoon apple, apricot, or pineapple preserves
- 1 teaspoon cinnamon sugar
- 1 teaspoon dark brown sugar
- 1 tablespoon finely chopped walnuts
- 16 golden raisins (optional)

Use a spoon or a pastry brush to spread the preserves across the entire surface of the dough. Sprinkle the cinnamon sugar evenly over the dough on top of the preserves. Sprinkle the brown sugar and nuts evenly over the dough.

Use a pizza cutter or knife to first cut the dough in half lengthwise. Then cut across horizontally. Then cut across on each diagonal. Your dough pieces will each look like a slice of pizza. Place 2 raisins toward the top (wide part) of each wedge. Follow the remaining instructions in the Ruggies recipe above for rolling and baking.

*notes*

## Hazelnut-Chocolate Ruggie Filling

**FILLS 8 RUGGIES**

1 to 2 tablespoons Nutella spread

1     teaspoon cinnamon sugar

1     tablespoon finely chopped walnuts

16    white chocolate chips

8     milk chocolate chips

In a glass bowl or other microwave-safe dish, heat the Nutella on high power for 10 seconds. Use a small spatula or a pastry brush to spread the Nutella across the entire surface of the dough. Sprinkle the cinnamon sugar evenly on top of the Nutella. Sprinkle the nuts over the top of the dough.

Use a pizza cutter to first cut the dough in half lengthwise. Then cut across horizontally. Then cut across on each diagonal. Your dough pieces will each look like a slice of pizza. Place 2 white chocolate chips and 1 milk chocolate chip toward the top of each wedge. Follow the remaining instructions in the Ruggies recipe above for rolling and baking.

*notes* _____

_____

_____

# Railroad Track Cookies

*Submitted by Missy Kolsky*
*From her grandmother Mary Margaret Mingst's recipe, San Francisco, California*

Missy Kolsky fondly remembers her grandmother "Gigi" as an amazing cook and a gifted baker. She was renowned for her wafer-thin sugar cookies made with a cookie press to resemble railroad tracks. Gigi made these any time the grandkids came to visit in San Francisco.

The preparation leading up to making the cookies was a big to-do. Gigi removed the butter from the refrigerator the night before, purchased baker's sugar, set the sifter on the countertop, and fitted the cookie press with the zigzag disk. There was an art to making these cookies, and the taste was pure satisfaction.

As a teen, Missy went to sleepaway camp, where she was handed a large parcel during mail call. Inside, packed in a decorative tin layered with waxed paper, were Railroad Track Cookies. Missy became quite the popular cabin mate! Now a parent herself, Missy appreciates Gigi's effort to send comforts of home, even from far away. Attention, campers—be on the lookout at mail call.

{ *. . . Missy went to sleepaway camp, where she was handed a large parcel during mail call . . . [she] became quite the popular cabin mate!*

# Railroad Track Cookies MAKES 4 TO 5 DOZEN COOKIES

2 cups all-purpose flour

¼ teaspoon baking soda

1 cup (2 sticks) butter, at room temperature

1 cup superfine granulated sugar (Missy uses C&H Baker's Sugar)

1 large egg

1 tablespoon vanilla or almond extract

Care package

Preheat the oven to 375°F. Line a baking sheet with parchment paper (or use nonstick spray). In a large bowl, whisk together the flour and baking soda. Set aside. Place the butter and sugar in the bowl of a stand mixer fitted with the paddle attachment and beat on medium speed until creamy. Reduce the speed to low and add the egg and vanilla. Add the flour mixture, a little at a time, and blend until smooth.

Following the manufacturer's directions, fit a cookie press with the disk that has what looks like a straight line with ridges on one side. Press the dough into the cookie press, making sure there are no air bubbles. Squeeze the dough through the press onto the baking sheet into three long strips vertically down the sheet, setting them at least 1 inch apart. The strips will look like railroad tracks. Bake for 8 to 10 minutes, until the cookies begin to brown at the edges. Remove from the oven and immediately cut the long strips into pieces about every 3 inches while the cookies are still soft. Cool for 1 minute, then transfer to a wire rack to let cool completely.

## SUGAR MOMMAS TIPS

*sugar mommas note:* To make your own superfine sugar, place granulated sugar in a food processor and pulse for 15 to 20 seconds.

*sugar mommas nifty gadget:* We suggest Wilton Comfort Grip cookie press.

# Kossuth Cakes

*Submitted by Mary-Louise Leipheimer, Foxcroft School*
*From Charlotte Haxall Noland's recipe, Middleburg, Virginia*

Legend has it that Kossuth Cakes were named after General Lajos Kossuth, who led the Hungarian Revolution of 1848. His country won independence in 1849. Thereafter, General Kossuth came to America and visited Baltimore in 1851. At some point, Kossuth Cakes appeared at St. Timothy's School in Stevenson, Baltimore County, Maryland. One can only assume that Miss Charlotte Haxall Noland enjoyed the Kossuth Cakes she found at St. Timothy's.

According to the December 9, 1929, issue of *TIME* magazine, Miss Noland taught "physical culture" at St. Timothy's School until moving to Virginia to start a camp. In 1914, due to the outbreak of WWI, "Miss Charlotte" founded Foxcroft School for girls. It was in Foxcroft memorabilia that we discovered this recipe for Kossuth Cakes.

While playing "documentary girls," we spoke with Ms. Sallie B. Summers, a cook at Foxcroft School for 36 years alongside Mr. Wallace Robinson. Sallie remembers making Kossuth Cakes for "big" occasions such as banquets, parents' weekends, and board meetings. She said that Mr. Wallace had the recipe and after he passed away in 1972, Kossuth Cakes were no longer made.

Sallie retired in 1982 and recently celebrated her ninety-fourth birthday. We asked Ms. Sallie if she remembers the schoolgirls doing mischievous things. She giggled and said she sure did, but she didn't care to talk about such things. Ms. Sallie is the keeper of the secrets.

Sallie's daughter, Sarah Thompson, took over as the cook when Ms. Sallie retired. Sarah began working at Foxcroft at age 15 and confirmed she knew about the Kossuth Cakes, but she never made them during her 57-year reign as queen of the kitchen. Mr. Mike Brown took over after Ms. Sarah retired in June 2009. He has been cooking in the Foxcroft kitchen since 2005. Mr. Brown has never seen a Kossuth Cake or the recipe.

We have resurrected Kossuth Cakes. These pastries are spongy vanilla cookie sandwiches filled with cream and drizzled with chocolate. We assume they were taken with tea or eaten during celebrations. Harken back to the late nineteenth century and enjoy this delicacy.

# Kossuth Cakes MAKES 12 TO 15 SANDWICH COOKIES

3   large eggs, separated (see Sugar Mommas Note)

⅓   cup all-purpose flour

⅛   teaspoon salt

⅓   cup granulated sugar

½   teaspoon vanilla extract

1   batch Kossuth Cake Cream Filling (recipe follows)

1   batch warm Kossuth Cake Chocolate Frosting (recipe follows)

Fox hunt

Preheat the oven to 425°F. Line a baking sheet with parchment paper (or use nonstick cooking spray). In a medium bowl, beat the egg whites with a handheld electric mixer on medium-high speed until stiff peaks form. Set aside. In a small bowl, whisk together the flour and salt. Set aside. Place 2 of the egg yolks and the sugar in the bowl of a stand mixer fitted with the paddle attachment and beat on medium-low speed until light colored, about 1 minute. Add in the vanilla and mix well. Add the flour mixture, a little at a time, until just blended. Use a spatula or wooden spoon to gently fold in the egg whites and stir until the mixture is smooth. Do not overmix (see Sugar Mommas Alert). The dough will be very light and airy.

Drop the dough onto the baking sheet by heaping teaspoonfuls, leaving at least 2 inches between cookies. Immediately place the baking sheet in the hot oven so the dough does not deflate. The cookies will round out and rise. Bake for 6 to 8 minutes, until the cookies are slightly brown around the edges. Remove from oven and cool for 1 minute. Transfer to a wire rack to let cool completely.

To assemble the cookies, transfer them to a piece of parchment paper on your work surface. Drizzle Kossuth Cake Chocolate Frosting over half of the cookies (flat side down) and set aside. Place one plain cookie on the work surface, flat side up. Top the cookie liberally with filling. Place a chocolate-coated cookie on top, flat side down. Transfer the assembled Kossuth Cakes to a platter or tray and chill in the refrigerator for at least 1 hour or up to overnight. Serve cold.

## Kossuth Cake Cream Filling

1 **cup heavy whipping cream**

¼ **cup granulated sugar**

½ **teaspoon vanilla extract**

Place the cream, sugar, and vanilla in
the bowl of a stand mixer fitted with
the whisk attachment. Beat on medium
speed until soft peaks form. Place
the filling in the refrigerator until the
cookies are cooled.

*notes* _____

_____

_____

_____

_____

_____

_____

_____

_____

***sugar mommas note:*** Three egg
whites and two egg yolks are used in
the cookie dough. You will also need two
egg yolks for the frosting. This means
four eggs total, and you will be left with
one unused egg white, which you can
scramble for breakfast.

***sugar mommas alert:*** When we say to
fold in the egg whites, we mean remove
the bowl from the stand and use a spatula or wooden spoon. Resist the temp-
tation to beat in the egg whites gently
on the lowest mixer setting. Trust us.
In this recipe, you actually have to follow the directions exactly, to the letter.
Figures . . . it comes from a school.

***old school:*** Wow your friends with this
dessert at the next luncheon. According to our research, this recipe has not
been prepared since the early 1970s. It's
a good bet your gal pals have never seen
these beauties before.

Try assembling the cookies in a baking cup using only unfrosted cookies.
Drizzle the frosting on top, allowing the
chocolate to drip down the sides and
pool at the bottom. After chilling, you
may then eat these foxy pastries from
the baking cup with a spoon so you
appear proper and ladylike.

## Kossuth Cake
## Chocolate Frosting

2½  ounces bittersweet chocolate

¼  cup (½ stick) butter

2⅓  cups confectioners' sugar

3  tablespoons hot water, or more as needed

2  egg yolks, beaten (one leftover from the dough recipe)

½  teaspoon vanilla extract

⅛  teaspoon salt

Place the chocolate and butter in the top of a double boiler (or in a metal bowl nestled in a saucepan of boiling water) over medium heat, stirring regularly. When the chocolate is melted, stir in the sugar. Add the hot water, 1 tablespoon at a time, mixing until smooth. Remove from the heat and gently mix in the egg yolks, vanilla, and salt, stirring after each addition. Blend with a handheld electric mixer on low speed (or by hand) for 1 minute, or until the frosting is smooth. If the frosting is too thick to pour, add more hot water, a little at a time, to achieve a consistency that allows for drizzling.

# schoolhouse *cookies*

*Submitted by Patricia ("Patsy") Manley Smith*
*(of SchoolHouse Kitchen), Norwich, New York*

Patsy's parents were Syracuse football fanatics (her father's alma mater), and the school played a big part in their lives. In fact, Manley Field House, located on campus, was named after Patsy's father.

When relaying this recipe to us, Patsy confessed a long-held family sugar secret. One day, while their parents attended a Syracuse game, the girls baked a cake. Someone forgot to include the sugar, and the dough became like a ball of mercury. They ended up throwing this "cake ball" all over the kitchen, even on the ceiling! When they were through playing, they had to start all over to bake a proper cake.

When their parents returned from the game, Patsy's father was perplexed about what could have possibly created those shiny circles on the ceiling. The sisters exchanged nervous glances as their father wondered aloud what on earth could have happened. Of course, the girls never spilled the beans . . . until now. Patsy couldn't recall what kind of cake it was, so she shared the following treasured family cookie recipes instead.

{
- Cream Cheese—Raspberry Pinwheels
- Chocolate Cloud Cookies

# Cream Cheese—
# Raspberry Pinwheels

*From Esther Ploucher Manley's recipe, Philadelphia, Pennsylvania*

These cookies originally appeared in the Manley household in the 1940s as a way of welcoming the children home from school or a vacation. They have been a family favorite for generations. Patsy's children fondly remember Wednesday-night dinners at their grandmother Esther's home during the 1970s and 1980s, when the cookies waited as a special treat, perfectly separated by layers of waxed paper in the cookie jar. Some had to be hidden away to ensure they weren't eaten too quickly.

This cookie is a frosted slice of flaky raspberry jelly roll. The light, buttery pastry with jam and nuts is terrific on its own, but with the vanilla icing slathered on, the cookies are heavenly. Today when Patsy's children have these cookies, they always think of their "Grammaman." Patsy's children are very sentimental about food and tradition, and she still welcomes them home with these delectable treats.

{ *Some had to be hidden away to ensure they weren't eaten too quickly.*

# Cream Cheese—Raspberry Pinwheels MAKES 2 TO 3 DOZEN PINWHEELS

2    cups all-purpose flour

¼    teaspoon salt

1    cup (2 sticks) butter, at room temperature

1    (8-ounce) package cream cheese

½    cup raspberry jelly or jam

⅓    cup chopped walnuts

1    warm batch Raspberry Pinwheel Vanilla Icing (recipe follows)

Hump day

**Day 1:** In a medium bowl, whisk together the flour and salt. Set aside. Place the butter and cream cheese in the bowl of a stand mixer fitted with the paddle attachment and beat on medium speed until creamy. Reduce the speed to low and add the flour mixture, a little at a time. Blend until smooth. Form the dough into a ball and cover tightly with plastic wrap. Chill in the refrigerator overnight (see Carpool Crunch).

**Day 2:** Remove the dough from the refrigerator. Place a piece of parchment paper on a work surface and dust with flour. Place the dough on the floured surface and roll out into an oblong shape about ⅛ inch thick (about the size of a 13 by 9-inch baking dish). Spread the jelly evenly over the dough surface, stopping ½ to ¾ inch from the edges. Sprinkle the walnuts evenly over the top. Starting with the long side closest to you, roll the dough away from you, using the parchment paper to wrap it, forming a tight tube or jelly roll. Pinch the seams and ends together to prevent leakage and fold the excess parchment paper over the ends. Cover tightly with plastic wrap and chill in the refrigerator for at least 2 hours.

Preheat the oven to 400°F. Line baking sheets with parchment paper (or use nonstick cooking spray). Remove the dough roll from the refrigerator and cut it into slices about ¼ inch thick. Place the slices on the baking sheets, leaving about 2 inches between cookies. Bake for 12 to 14 minutes, until light golden brown. Make the icing while the cookies bake.

Remove the cookies from the oven and cool for 1 minute. Lift the edges of the parchment paper and transfer the entire sheet of cookies (still on the paper) to a wire rack. If you did not bake the cookies on parchment paper, place wax paper on the rack to keep the icing from dripping all over, and transfer the cookies individually. Spread the icing on top of the cookies while they are still slightly warm, then let cool completely.

## Raspberry Pinwheel
Vanilla Icing

2   tablespoons (¼ stick) butter, at room temperature

2   cups confectioners' sugar

1   teaspoon vanilla extract

2   tablespoons boiling water, or more as needed

Place the butter, sugar, and vanilla in the bowl of a stand mixer fitted with the paddle attachment and beat on medium speed until creamy. Add the water, a little at a time, until the icing reaches your desired consistency (similar to the icing on a cinnamon roll).

*notes*

*carpool crunch:* If you have room in the refrigerator for a long, flat object, you may roll the dough out on Day 1 and then chill it overnight. Place waxed or parchment paper on a clean surface and dust lightly with flour. Place the dough on the floured surface and roll out into an oblong shape about ⅛ inch thick (about the size of a 13 by 9-inch baking dish). Lightly dust the top of the dough with flour and then cover with another sheet of waxed or parchment paper. Cover tightly with plastic wrap and place the flat dough in the refrigerator to chill overnight. On Day 2, you can skip right to the jam-spreading step.

*sass it up:* Try apricot jam or blackberry preserves instead of raspberry. If you're craving chocolate, spread the dough with Nutella. Sprinkle cinnamon sugar over the filling before rolling, or try brown sugar for variety.

# Chocolate Cloud Cookies

*From Lena Manley Flanagan's recipe (via Regina Nelson), Norwich, New York*

These cookies were given to Patsy's paternal aunt, Lena Manley Flanagan, in the early 1930s by the lovely Regina Nelson. The Nelsons and Manleys have remained family friends for four generations. The cookies were made fairly often, as Patsy usually requested anything chocolate. These double-chocolate cookies have a shiny chocolate icing and are superb with or without nuts.

Chocolate Cloud Cookies were truly a find because we have never tasted anything like it. This cookie simulates chocolate air. We paired it with a rich fudge frosting: The combination of light and dense makes for a uniquely scrumptious delight.

{ *Place an espresso bean on top of each cookie after icing for visual effect.*

# Chocolate Cloud Cookies MAKES ABOUT 3 DOZEN COOKIES

½ cup whole milk

½ teaspoon baking soda

1½ cups all-purpose flour

1 teaspoon baking powder

1 cup packed dark brown sugar

½ cup (1 stick) butter, at room temperature

1 large egg

1 teaspoon vanilla extract

2 ounces unsweetened chocolate, melted

1 warm batch Kossuth Cake Chocolate Frosting (page 168)

Doppler radar

Preheat the oven to 350°F. Line a baking sheet with parchment paper (or use nonstick cooking spray). In a medium bowl, whisk together the milk and baking soda until all lumps are dissolved. Set aside. In a large bowl, whisk together the flour and baking powder. Set aside.

Place the sugar and butter in the bowl of a stand mixer fitted with the paddle attachment and beat on medium speed until creamy. Reduce the speed to low and add the egg and vanilla. Add the melted chocolate and mix until smooth. Add half of the flour mixture and blend. Slowly incorporate the milk mixture. Add the second half of the flour mixture and blend until smooth.

Drop the dough by heaping teaspoonfuls onto the baking sheet, leaving at least 1 inch between cookies. Bake for 8 to 10 minutes, until the cookies spring back when touched. Make the frosting while the cookies bake. Remove the cookies from the oven and cool for 1 minute.

Lift the edges of the parchment paper and transfer the entire sheet of cookies (still on the paper) to a wire rack. If you did not bake the cookies on parchment paper, place wax paper on the rack to keep the frosting from dripping all over, and transfer the cookies individually. While the cookies are still warm, drizzle a teaspoon of the chocolate frosting on each and use the back of a spoon to spread the icing around. We like to keep some of the underlying cookie exposed because it is so unusual. Let cool until the frosting sets.

# Cakies

*Submitted by Tiffany Lemons*
*From her mother Bonnie Smith's recipe, Tucson, Arizona*

Tiffany Lemons's three little girls stand in matching holiday dresses in front of their open closet preparing for the big event. Red, pink, and purple shoes sparkle at them from the shelves, but they carefully select the black patent leather shoes, along with pearl necklaces. Tiffany frantically completes the final preparations for the annual mother-daughter cookie exchange.

Tiffany's mother, Bonnie, started this tradition in Arizona, where Bonnie hosted the annual event. Tiffany helped her mother make the Cakies, then dressed in her black patent shoes and pearls. Bonnie invited her girlfriends and their daughters. Each invitee brought three dozen cookies, which were arranged on the dining room table. Guests took platters around the room, collecting samples from every tray. There was the usual assortment of snickerdoodles, snowballs, peppermint bark, toffee, and chocolate chip cookies, but the Cakies were the most sought after. After enjoying some tea, coffee, or lemonade, and conversation, each mother-daughter set went home with three dozen cookies to enjoy during the holidays.

Tiffany moved to California and started the Cakies ritual when her eldest daughter turned two years old. Rules are rules, and according to tradition, this is a girls-only event. No boys allowed. She hopes that, in 20+ years, her daughters will carry on the Cakies tradition. She looks forward to the day her girls call her at midnight asking those familiar questions, comparing techniques, frosting the final batch, and anxiously arranging last-minute party preparations.

{ *Rules are rules, and according to tradition, this is a girls-only event.*

# Cakies MAKES ABOUT 6 DOZEN CAKIES

½ cup vegetable shortening (we suggest Crisco Butter Flavor)

1 cup packed light brown sugar

½ cup granulated sugar

2 large eggs

1 cup sour cream

1 teaspoon vanilla extract

2¾ cups all-purpose flour

½ teaspoon baking soda

1 teaspoon salt

1 batch Cakies Frosting (recipe follows)

Sprinkles or other decorations

Black patent leather shoes

**Day 1:** Place the shortening and sugars in the bowl of a stand mixer fitted with the paddle attachment and beat on medium speed until creamy. Reduce the speed to low and blend in the eggs, one at a time. Add the sour cream, blending until just combined. Add the vanilla and mix until smooth, about 1 minute. Cover tightly with plastic wrap and chill in the refrigerator overnight.

**Day 2:** In a large bowl, whisk the flour, baking soda, and salt. Set aside. Return the shortening and sugar mixture bowl from the refrigerator to the mixing stand. With the mixer on low speed, blend in the flour mixture, a little at a time, until just incorporated. The cookie dough will look like thick and sticky tapioca pudding. Cover tightly with plastic wrap and return to the refrigerator to chill for at least 4 hours (or see Old School tip).

Preheat the oven to 375°F. Line baking sheets with parchment paper (or use nonstick cooking spray). When the cookie dough is cold, drop it by rounded tablespoonfuls onto the baking sheets, leaving about 2 inches between cookies. Place the remaining dough in the refrigerator between batches to keep it chilled. Bake for 11 to 13 minutes, until the cookies begin to turn golden. Remove from the oven and cool for 2 minutes. Transfer to a wire rack to let cool completely.

Spread the frosting onto the cooled cookies. Add colored sugar crystals or other decorations while the frosting is warm.

## Cakies Frosting

**2 cups confectioners' sugar**

**½ cup (1 stick) butter, melted**

**1 teaspoon vanilla extract**

**2 to 4 tablespoons hot water**

Place the confectioners' sugar in the bowl of a stand mixer fitted with the whisk attachment. Slowly add the butter and vanilla and mix on medium-low speed until well combined, about 1 minute. Add 2 tablespoons water and mix until blended. Add more water 1 tablespoon at a time, if needed, to achieve the desired consistency (thick enough to spread).

## SUGAR MOMMAS TIPS

*sugar mommas notes:* There are rules for a successful cookie exchange. Follow Wilton's book, *Wilton Cookie Exchange,* or go online to the Martha Stewart Cookie-Swap Party Planner. Use these guidelines or create traditions of your own.

Drop by your local discount store once in a while to pick up festive platters, boxes, or tins, and colored cellophane wrap, and ribbons so guests can transport their loot home in pretty packages.

*sass it up:* Be the sassiest gal at the party by bringing the best hostess gift. If you want to outshine the other moms, bring decorative, food-safe parchment paper to line the trays or package the cookies. Wilton sells holiday-themed sheets. What a find!

*modern variations:* Tiffany's daughters were the first to use sprinkles to decorate their Cakies. Use pearlized sprinkles to get a bold dash of color in the form of colored mini beads. In the holiday spirit? Use red, white, and green crystals or sprinkles in the shape of trees, snowflakes, or Gingerbread Boys.

For colored frosting, add food coloring, one drop at a time, to get your desired tint.

*old school:* According to the original instructions, the recipe was made in 3 days. You would combine the wet ingredients first and chill overnight. Then you would add in the dry ingredients, blend, and chill again overnight. On the third day, you would bake and frost. This recipe is about tradition—following in the footsteps of Bonnie is what binds these ladies together. Nevertheless, we tried to accelerate the process for you.

# Molasses Construction Crumples

*Submitted by Keith Christensen*
*From his grandmother Bertha Blausey's recipe, Quincy, Illinois*

The most extraordinary thing that happened to me (Momma Reiner) in the spring of 2010 was that the water main on my street broke. The original line was put in around 1920, and every couple of months, it would spring a new leak. At increasingly inconvenient times (such as Christmas Day), the water and power company came out, shut off the water, and conducted a repair. This is the way it had been for 10 years.

Unexpectedly, the City of Angels decided to replace the entire water line down our street. This utility project was expected to take a minimum of two months, required the water to be shut off intermittently, and forced the street to be closed to vehicles. Perfect timing. The construction took place at precisely the same time I was testing recipes for this book. How could I bake without water? How would I carry 100 pounds of flour to the house if I had to park a half mile away? I had to see what I could do to make life more convenient and not miss my deadlines.

I went outside to chat with "the guys" and tell them what I was up to. The Los Angeles Department of Water and Power employees were very interested that I would be baking sweets every day. I needed water; they enjoyed cookies. We struck a bargain and became fast friends. This relationship was mutually beneficial. Not only did I get water and access to my garage, but I also had built-in tasters just steps away from my front door. I brought my friends (with their drills, cranes, backhoes, and adorable construction uniforms) cookies every afternoon. The day they began calling me "Cookie Monster," I felt I had reached a new level of professional success.

Keith was assigned to this project. He was the first DWP employee to gamble his macho reputation and bring me his Grandma Blausey's recipe for Molasses Crumples. During a lunch break, Keith recounted his memories of making these cookies. He said, "If I was lucky, I got to help Grandma make them. The cool part was rolling the dough into a ball and smashing them down with a sugar-coated glass to flatten them. That was almost as good as eating them right out of the oven with a glass of milk." This event reassured me that most everyone has a special sugar something in his or her family.

When I told the guys we were moving on to bars (not the liquid kind), they responded, "Oh, good. We're getting sick of cookies." *That* made me laugh.

{ *"The day they began calling me 'Cookie Monster,' I felt I had reached a new level of professional success."*
—*Momma Reiner*

# Molasses Construction Crumples
**MAKES ABOUT 4 DOZEN COOKIES**

2¼ cups all-purpose flour

2 teaspoons baking soda

1 teaspoon ground cinnamon

1 teaspoon ground ginger

½ teaspoon ground cloves

¼ teaspoon salt

¾ cup vegetable shortening

1 cup packed light brown sugar

1 large egg

¼ cup molasses

1 cup granulated sugar, for rolling

Hard hat

In a large bowl, whisk together the flour, baking soda, cinnamon, ginger, cloves, and salt. Set aside. Place the shortening and brown sugar in the bowl of a stand mixer fitted with the paddle attachment and beat on medium speed until light and fluffy, about 2 minutes. Mix in the egg and molasses on low speed until blended. Add the flour mixture, a little at a time, and beat until the flour is just incorporated, about 1 minute. Form the dough into a ball and cover tightly with plastic wrap. Chill in the refrigerator for at least 2 hours.

Preheat the oven to 375°F. Line baking sheets with parchment paper (or use nonstick cooking spray). Place the granulated sugar in a small bowl and set aside. Once the dough is chilled, roll a heaping tablespoonful of dough into a ball the size of a large walnut. Dip the top half in sugar, and place it sugar side up on a baking sheet (see Old School tip). Repeat with the remaining dough, leaving 2 inches between cookies.

Bake for 10 to 12 minutes, until the cookies are set but soft in the center. Be careful not to overbake them. Remove from the oven and cool for 1 minute. Transfer to a wire rack to let cool completely.

*notes*

CHAPTER
5

# cool bars and summer stars

Before this book, the mention of bars called to mind a glass of Pinot Noir or a Mandarin Cosmopolitan. We were so focused on our cookie repertoire that we almost missed an entire subdivision of confection. Open yourself up to a new sugar category and invite crisps, cobblers, and bars in! You'll be pleasantly surprised by how easy these sweets are to assemble.

The recipes in this chapter can be made any time of year, but we think they are ideal for summer BBQs. Congo Bars, Oatmeal Carmelitas, Apple Crisp, and Peach Queen Cobbler all serve many and can be made in advance. Dust off your baking dishes and place them within reach for the spontaneous company that is sure to drop by when they smell the aromas emanating from your house. Bars, crisps, and cobblers allow you to enjoy your summer and entertain effortlessly until it's time to retire the white shoes.

Oh, yeah—don't forget the ice cream.

# Oatmeal Carmelitas

*Submitted by Debbie Carpenter*
*From her grandmother Vina Marie Post's recipe, Madison, Wisconsin*

Grandma and Grandpa Post traveled in their trailer each winter in search of warm weather and a golf course. During the summer, they settled the RV in a park near Lake Mendota. When the grandkids came to visit Madison in the 1960s, Grandma Post let Debbie and her sisters sleep in the motor home. Nothing could be neater to a kid!

In his spare time, Grandpa Post built bicycles, and the kids were always riding around the trailer park on funky-looking bikes he'd pieced together. Debbie's favorite was the tandem bike he made with her older sister Kathy. Nothing quite matched the freedom the freckle-faced girls enjoyed while cruising around on bikes in the summer months without a care in the world.

> *Oozing caramel, chocolate, and pecans between layers of crunchy oatmeal, they instantly became Debbie's favorite . . .*

In between adventures, Grandma Post and the girls would stroll over to the Piggly Wiggly to buy the ingredients necessary to make Oatmeal Carmelitas. Oozing caramel, chocolate, and pecans between layers of crunchy oatmeal, they instantly became Debbie's favorite, and Grandma Post always had the cookie jar filled with them for the girls to enjoy.

Grandma Post was also skilled at knitting and crocheting. When Debbie was a teenager, she found a picture in a magazine of a knit halter top with a watermelon on the front. Grandma Post knitted the top and surprised Debbie on her next summer visit. Debbie wore that shirt to shreds. We can easily imagine Debbie riding a handcrafted bike in the spiffy yellow halter with a big watermelon on the front eating Oatmeal Carmelitas.

Grandma Post lived to be 99 years old. She passed away one month before her 100th birthday. Her Carmelitas are so good, we expect the recipe to survive well beyond another 100 years.

# Oatmeal Carmelitas
MAKES ABOUT 2 DOZEN 2-INCH SQUARE BARS

**(MOMMA REINER'S PREFERRED BAR)**

| | |
|---|---|
| 2 cups all-purpose flour | 1 (14-ounce) bag Kraft soft caramel candies, unwrapped (about 50) |
| 1 teaspoon baking soda | ½ cup evaporated milk |
| ½ teaspoon salt | 1 cup semisweet chocolate chips |
| 1 cup (2 sticks) butter, at room temperature | 1 cup chopped pecans (optional) |
| 1½ cups packed light brown sugar | *Tiger Beat* magazine |
| 2 cups quick-cooking oats | |

Preheat the oven to 350°F. Grease a 9 by 13-inch baking dish (or use nonstick baking spray). Set aside.

In a large bowl, whisk together the flour, baking soda, and salt. Set aside. Place the butter and brown sugar in the bowl of a stand mixer fitted with the paddle attachment and beat on medium speed until creamy. Slowly add the flour mixture and blend until incorporated. Use a wooden spoon or spatula to fold in the oats. The mixture will be crumbly. Transfer half (about 3 cups) of the mixture to the baking dish. Use your fingers to gently press and spread the mixture evenly on the bottom of the baking dish. Bake for 10 minutes to set.

While the first layer is baking, place the caramels and milk in a small saucepan (or see Carpool Crunch). Cook over medium-low heat, stirring constantly, until the caramels are melted. Remove from the heat and let cool slightly.

Remove the crust from the oven. Sprinkle the chocolate chips and pecans (if desired) evenly over the top. Carefully pour the caramel mixture on top of the chocolate chips and nuts, and spread evenly. Sprinkle the remaining crumb mixture over the top. Bake for 15 to 20 minutes, until lightly browned. Remove from the oven and let cool to room temperature. Then refrigerate for at least 2 hours, or until the bars are set. Cut into 2-inch squares.

_____

_____

_____

_____

_____

_____

_____

_____

_____

_____

## SUGAR MOMMAS TIPS

*sugar mommas notes:* If you are a true caramel lover, forego the chocolate chips and nuts to have a pure caramel encounter.

When you remove the baking dish from the oven, don't put it in the fridge. Run to the freezer, grab some vanilla ice cream, and drop chunks of the warm, gooey Carmelitas over the ice cream. Whatever you do, take a moment to enjoy the gooey phase before the (refrigerated) solid phase.

*carpool crunch:* Use Kraft Premium Caramel Bits—already unwrapped for easy melting.

Place the caramels and evaporated milk in a glass or other microwave-safe bowl. Heat on high power for 2 minutes. Stir and repeat in 30-second increments until the caramel is melted and has a smooth consistency.

# Chocolate-Toffee-Caramel Bars

*Submitted by Lisa Rocchio*
*From her mother-in-law Joan Crowley Rocchio's recipe, Saginaw, Michigan*

Joan Crowley Rocchio was an impressive figure even before she was introduced to her future daughter-in-law. In the early days of courtship with Joan's son John, Lisa Rocchio often heard about John's mother's magnificent baking. When John first brought Lisa home to meet his family, she was welcomed with these outrageous Chocolate-Toffee-Caramel Bars. Joan warned Lisa that the bars were so rich that she should take only a small bite. The sweet treats were just too devilishly good to practice any type of civility or self-control. Imagine the first impression Lisa made when she gobbled up half the platter!

When Joan passed away, Lisa wanted to honor her appropriately. After Joan's funeral, Lisa decided to surprise John's six siblings by bringing Chocolate-Toffee-Caramel Bars to the reception. She proudly carried her tray to the dining area as she watched others juggling their dishes. When the food was laid out on tables, Lisa realized that several family members arrived with one of Joan's famous recipes. What a fitting tribute to Joan—a baker at heart.

{ *The sweet treats were just too devilishly good to practice any type of civility or self-control.*

# Chocolate-Toffee-Caramel Bars MAKES ABOUT 2 DOZEN 2-INCH SQUARE BARS

1 (18.25-ounce) box yellow cake mix (Lisa uses Pillsbury Moist Supreme Golden Butter Cake Mix)

1/3 cup vegetable oil

2 large eggs

1 (12-ounce) package semisweet chocolate chips

1 cup white chocolate chips

1 cup crushed Heath bars (or Heath Milk Chocolate Toffee Bits)

1/2 cup (1 stick) butter, at room temperature

32 Kraft soft caramel candies, unwrapped (or Kraft Premium Caramel Bits)

1 (14-ounce) can sweetened condensed milk

Self-restraint

Preheat the oven to 350°F. Grease a 9 by 13-inch baking dish (or use nonstick cooking spray). Place the cake mix, oil, and eggs in a large bowl and mix well. Use a wooden spoon or spatula to fold in the semisweet chocolate chips, white chocolate chips, and Heath bits. Press half of the mixture (about 3 cups) into the bottom of the baking dish. Bake for 10 minutes.

While the crust is baking, place the butter, caramels, and condensed milk in a medium saucepan (or see Carpool Crunch). Cook over medium-low heat, stirring constantly, until the caramels are melted and the mixture is smooth. Remove the crust from the oven and slowly pour the caramel mixture over the top. Top with the remaining cake mixture and spread evenly.

Bake for 25 to 30 minutes, until the top is set and deep golden brown. Remove from the oven and let cool for 20 minutes. Run a knife around the sides of the dish to loosen. Let cool for an additional 40 minutes, then refrigerate for at least 1 hour, or until the bars are set. Cut into 2-inch squares.

*notes* _____

_____

_____

_____

_____

_____

_____

_____

_____

_____

_____

_____

_____

*carpool crunch:* Place the butter, caramels, and condensed milk in a glass or other microwave-safe bowl. Heat on high power for 2 minutes. Stir and repeat in 30-second increments until the caramel is melted and has a smooth consistency.

# Kentucky Derby Bars

*Submitted by Lisa Rocchio*
*From her friend Missy Bailey Massa's recipe, Mobile, Alabama*

Missy Bailey Massa introduced her roommate, Lisa Rocchio, to Derby-Pie while they were students at the University of Alabama. Missy whipped up her hometown pie for every special occasion and for no reason at all. Lisa brought the recipe with her to the West Coast and made it anytime a dessert was needed. Friends went crazy for it, but Lisa noticed that some people did not want an entire slice of pie. She became a baking pioneer, changing the crust and converting the pie into bars for smaller servings. These Kentucky Derby Bars are a Triple Crown winner!

{ *These Kentucky Derby Bars are a Triple Crown winner!*

# Kentucky Derby Bars MAKES ABOUT 2 DOZEN 2-INCH SQUARE BARS

## GRAHAM CRACKER CRUST

2   cups graham cracker crumbs

½   cup (1 stick) butter, melted

## FILLING

1   cup granulated sugar

½   cup (1 stick) butter, melted and cooled

2   large eggs

1   teaspoon vanilla extract

½   cup all-purpose flour

1   cup chopped pecans

1   cup semisweet chocolate chips

Run for the Roses

Preheat the oven to 325°F. Butter a 9 by 13-inch baking dish (or use nonstick cooking spray).

**To make the crust:** Place the graham cracker crumbs and butter in the bowl of a food processor. Pulse several times until the mixture forms moist crumbs. Press the mixture firmly and evenly on the bottom of the baking dish and set aside.

**To make the filling:** Place the sugar and butter in the bowl of a stand mixer fitted with the paddle attachment and beat on medium speed until combined. Reduce the mixer speed to low and add the eggs, one at a time, and the vanilla. Gradually add the flour and mix until just combined. Use a wooden spoon or spatula to fold in the pecans and chocolate chips. Pour the filling on top of the crust and spread it evenly.

Bake for 33 to 38 minutes, until the bars begin to turn golden brown. Remove from the oven and let cool for 10 to 15 minutes before serving. Cut into 2-inch squares. In Lisa's own words, "You want them gooey, but not too gooey." Sugar Mommas Interpretation: Pull them out of the oven a smidge undercooked so that they don't dry out.

_notes_

_sass it up:_ Add 3 or 4 tablespoons of bourbon to the filling after you have mixed in the vanilla to solidify your Dixie experience. We used Maker's Mark.

For chocolate chips, we used Cacao Barry mini semisweet chips.

_old school:_ To return this recipe to its original pie form, pour the filling into a 9-inch unbaked pie crust (not a graham cracker crust). Place the pie pan on a baking sheet and bake at 325°F for 45 to 50 minutes. Let cool for 2 hours. Serve with vanilla ice cream.

# Chocolate-Mint Bars

*Submitted by Robin Nelsen Meierhoff*
*From her grandmother Evelyn Newquist Nelsen's recipe, Duluth, Minnesota*

Evelyn Newquist Nelsen was delivered by a midwife at home on May 8, 1920, in Duluth's West End. She eventually married and raised two sons (including Robin's father) on Pike Lake.

Robin was Ev's first and only grandchild for 17 years, so she basked in uninterrupted attention. Although she could usually talk her grandparents into buying her the latest jeans or a cool pair of shoes, Robin claims she was spoiled not with material items but more so with bits of wisdom and unconditional love. Robin's parents were divorced when she was four years old, and she treasured time spent with her grandparents for the stability it provided. Robin and her grandmother formed a tight bond during the years they would sit drinking coffee and nibbling on baked goods during every visit. Robin cannot remember ever leaving Evelyn's home without Chocolate-Mint Bars, cookies, or a loaf of banana bread.

{ *Evelyn represents every grandmother who has stepped in to provide a source of love and wisdom in a grandchild's life.*

Today Robin's relationship with Ev is just as strong. They chat daily, arguing over politics and family drama. They always end their conversations with "I love you." At 90 years young, Evelyn is not just a grandmother but also a best girlfriend to Robin. Like so many women we have met along this journey, Evelyn represents every grandmother who has stepped in to provide a source of love and wisdom in a grandchild's life—like a sturdy support beam when the walls seem to cave in around us.

In Robin's own words, "I wish I had taken the time to bake with her, but I was too caught up in my own life. I'm afraid her skills, but not her recipes, will be lost when she is gone. These are my favorite bars of Ev's, and they are divine!"

# Chocolate-Mint Bars
### MAKES ABOUT 2 DOZEN 2-INCH SQUARE BARS
### (MOMMA JENNA'S PREFERRED BAR)

1   cup all-purpose flour

½   teaspoon salt

½   cup (1 stick) butter, at room temperature

1   cup granulated sugar

4   large eggs

1   (16-ounce) can chocolate syrup (Evelyn uses Hershey's; see Sugar Mommas Note)

1   teaspoon vanilla extract

1   batch Chocolate-Mint Filling, made while the bars cool (recipe follows)

1   batch Chocolate-Mint Glaze, made while the filling sets (recipe follows)

Phone call to your grandma

Preheat the oven to 350°F. Grease a 9 by 13-inch baking dish (or use nonstick cooking spray). Set aside.

In a small bowl, whisk together the flour and salt. Set aside. Place the butter and sugar in the bowl of a stand mixer fitted with the paddle attachment and beat on medium speed until creamy. Add the eggs, one at a time, blending well. Slowly add the flour mixture and blend on low speed until just incorporated. Add the chocolate syrup and vanilla and beat until the mixture is smooth. Pour the batter evenly into the baking dish. Bake for 25 to 30 minutes, until a toothpick inserted in the center comes out clean. Remove from the oven and let cool for 30 to 35 minutes.

While the bars are cooling, make the filling. Spread the filling evenly on top of the cooled cake layer, then let it stand while you prepare the glaze. When the filling is set, gently spread the glaze evenly on top of the filling. Place in the refrigerator and chill for 2 hours, or until the bars are set. Cut into 2-inch squares.

## Chocolate-Mint Filling

- ½ cup (1 stick) butter, at room temperature
- 2 cups confectioners' sugar
- 2 tablespoons milk
- ½ teaspoon peppermint extract

Place the butter and sugar in the bowl of a stand mixer fitted with the paddle attachment and beat on medium speed until creamy. Add the milk and peppermint extract and blend until light and fluffy.

## Chocolate-Mint Glaze

- 1 cup semisweet chocolate chips
- 6 tablespoons (¾ stick) butter, at room temperature

Place the chocolate chips and butter in a glass or other microwave-safe bowl. Microwave in 30-second intervals on high power until the chocolate is melted, stirring in between.

*notes* _____
_____
_____
_____
_____

## SUGAR MOMMAS TIPS

*sugar mommas notes:* If you can't find a 16-ounce can of chocolate syrup, use 1½ cups of any chocolate syrup.

Keep these bars refrigerated for a cool, refreshing treat!

*modern variation:* Spread the glaze on the bars before the filling sets. Use a knife to gently swirl the two layers together so that the filling will show through on top as the glaze hardens.

*old school:* Ev added 1 or 2 drops of green food coloring to the filling before spreading it.

*sass it up:* Sprinkle crushed mint candies on top or place a mini candy cane on each bar for a Christmas party.

# German Chocolate—Caramel Squares

*Submitted by Sue Marguleas*
*From her aunt Jan Hammes's recipe, Sterling, Illinois*

Jan Hammes made German Chocolate—Caramel Squares for every family event. She lived in Sterling, Illinois, and would bake them, pack them up, and bring them to holidays, reunions, and family gatherings at her parents' farm outside of La Crosse, Wisconsin. Eventually Jan's sister, Darlene, acquired the recipe so she could make the bars at home for her daughter Sue. Sue loved melting the caramels and stealing a lick from the spoon!

Darlene typed up the recipe for Sue when she left for college. In her freshman frenzy, Sue forgot about the recipe as well as the bars. Fifteen years later, Aunt Jan brought the German Chocolate—Caramel Squares to a reunion held in a coulee where Sue had played as a child. Sue squealed with delight and thanked her aunt with a bear hug for bringing back a piece of her childhood. When Sue returned home, she looked through her old blue recipe box and, sure enough, there was the typed recipe from her mother. On the back she had written, "Sue: This is the bar recipe you loved as a kid. Love, Mom." What sweet memory is waiting in your recipe box?

{ *Sue squealed with delight and thanked her aunt with a bear hug for bringing back a piece of her childhood.*

# German Chocolate—
# Caramel Squares MAKES ABOUT 2 DOZEN 2-INCH SQUARE BARS

1   (14-ounce) package Kraft soft caramel candies, unwrapped (about 50 pieces)

1/3   cup evaporated milk

1   (18.25-ounce) box German chocolate cake mix

1   tablespoon water

1/2   cup (1 stick) butter, melted

1   cup chopped walnuts

1   cup semisweet chocolate chips

3 by 5 recipe card

Preheat the oven to 350°F. Butter and flour a 9 by 13-inch baking dish (or use nonstick baking spray with flour). Set aside.

Place the caramels and milk in the top of a double boiler (or in a metal bowl nestled in a saucepan of boiling water) over medium heat (or see Carpool Crunch tip). Stir constantly until the caramels are melted. Remove the saucepan from the heat and set aside.

Place the cake mix, water, and melted butter in the bowl of a stand mixer fitted with the paddle attachment and beat on medium speed until well blended. Use a wooden spoon or spatula to fold in the walnuts. The mixture will be crumbly. Press half of the mixture firmly into the baking dish. Bake for 6 minutes, or until the crust is set. Remove from the oven. Sprinkle the chocolate chips over the crust while it is hot. Pour the caramel mixture over the chocolate. Sprinkle the remaining half of the crumble mixture on top. Bake for 18 minutes, or until the bars are set. Remove from the oven and let cool completely. Cut into 2-inch squares.

notes

_____
_____
_____
_____
_____
_____
_____
_____
_____
_____
_____
_____

*sass it up:* After the caramel layer, toss in some Heath bar bits or butterscotch chips before adding the final layer of cake batter.

*carpool crunch:* Instead of wrapped caramels, use Kraft Premium Caramel Bits—already unwrapped for easy melting.

To speed up the melting, place the caramels and evaporated milk in a glass or other microwave-safe bowl. Heat on high power for 2 minutes. Stir and repeat in 30-second increments until the caramel is melted and has a smooth consistency.

# Congo Bars

*Submitted by Maureen Murphy*
*From her mother Jean Murphy's recipe, Seattle, Washington*

Jean Murphy made these bars for her daughter Maureen and her three brothers at least once a week to take in school lunches, to eat when they came home after class, and for dessert. The scents wafting from Jean's kitchen must have alerted the entire neighborhood when a batch came out of the oven. All the local kids would drop by for a visit. As they walked through the kitchen, they would grab a bar from the big wooden cookie jar on the counter. Jean never complained that the kids ate all her bars. She was flattered that her baked goods were in demand.

Maureen's three sons loved Congo Bars as much as she did. Maureen's eldest son, Colin, included the recipe as part of his eighth-grade family genealogy project. What a novel idea—we think every ancestral study should include the family sweets!

{ *What a novel idea—we think every ancestral study should include the family sweets!*

# Congo Bars MAKES ABOUT 2 DOZEN 2-INCH SQUARE BARS

2 cups all-purpose flour

1 tablespoon baking powder

1 teaspoon salt

¾ cup (1½ sticks) butter, melted

1 (16-ounce) box light brown sugar

3 large eggs

1½ teaspoons vanilla extract

1 (12-ounce) package semisweet chocolate chips

1 cup chopped walnuts or pecans (optional)

Backpacks

Preheat the oven to 350°F. Grease a 9 by 13-inch baking dish (or use nonstick cooking spray). Set aside.

In a medium bowl, whisk together the flour, baking powder, and salt. Set aside. Place the butter and sugar in the bowl of a stand mixer fitted with the paddle attachment and beat on medium speed until combined. Reduce the speed to low and add the eggs, one at a time. Add the vanilla. Add the flour mixture, a little at a time, and blend until smooth. Use a wooden spoon or spatula to fold in the chocolate chips, and nuts, if desired.

Pour the batter into the baking dish. Bake for 30 to 35 minutes, until a toothpick inserted in the center comes out clean. Remove from the oven and let cool completely. Cut into 2-inch squares.

notes

*sugar mommas note:* These bars are delicious warm. If they get a bit dried out, wrap them in a damp paper towel and microwave on high power for 15 to 20 seconds. They will be revived as though fresh from the oven.

*sass it up:* Substitute all or part of the semisweet chocolate chips or nuts with butterscotch chips, white chocolate chips, caramel bits, or flaked coconut.

*old school:* Maureen used 67 percent cacao chips.

# Deer Angie's Brownies

*Submitted by Maurie Ankenman Cannon*
*From Angie Hall's recipe, St. Louis, Missouri*

Angie Hall was the longtime housekeeper in Maurie Ankenman's family. Maurie remembers Angie as a better-than-average cook, and she still returns to many of Angie's recipes, such as these brownies. Maurie's husband aptly described these treats as soft and cake-like, "with a firm icing that literally melts between your lips and the back of your tongue." Brownies seem relatively commonplace, but Angie's brownies will bring you to your knees!

We can attest that Angie's brownies are favored by creatures great and small. Momma Reiner made these treats for her son's baseball team picnic. The moms laid out quite a spread at the local park, a retreat in the midst of the Los Angeles urban setting. Three hillside picnic tables, covered in a banquet fit for royalty, sat waiting for the game's end. We were focused on watching fathers and sons engage in America's favorite pastime.

As the ninth inning neared its close, we glanced over toward the feast. A surprise guest was in attendance—a deer had ventured out from the trees. With a veritable buffet in front of him, and with no mind to the baseballs flying through the air, he stood leisurely eating the platter of brownies. All eyes were on that deer, who could not be bothered to step aside until the entire tray was consumed. You have been warned . . . grab a brownie while you can.

> With a veritable buffet in front of him, and with no mind to the baseballs flying through the air, [the deer] stood leisurely eating the platter of brownies.

# Deer Angie's
# Brownies MAKES ABOUT 2 DOZEN (1- TO 2-INCH) SQUARE BROWNIES

1    cup (2 sticks) butter, at room
     temperature

4    ounces unsweetened chocolate

4    large eggs

2    cups granulated sugar

1    teaspoon vanilla extract

1    cup all-purpose flour

1    cup finely chopped pecans
     (optional)

1    batch warm Deer Angie's Brownie
     Icing (recipe follows)

     Deer repellent

Preheat the oven to 325°F. Lightly grease two 9-inch square baking dishes (or use nonstick cooking spray). Set aside.

Place the butter and chocolate in the top of a double boiler (or in a metal bowl nestled in a saucepan of water) over medium-low heat (or see Carpool Crunch tip). Stir constantly until the chocolate is melted. Remove from the heat.

 Place the eggs and sugar in the bowl of a stand mixer fitted with the paddle attachment and beat on medium speed until well blended, about 1 minute. Add the vanilla. Add the chocolate mixture very slowly (you want to temper, not cook, the eggs), blending well. Add the flour and blend on low speed until just combined. Use a wooden spoon or spatula to fold in the pecans, if desired.

Divide the batter evenly between the baking dishes and bake for 22 to 25 minutes, until a toothpick inserted in the center comes out clean. Remove from the oven and let cool completely in the dishes.

While the brownies bake, make the icing. Use a knife or angled spatula to spread the frosting on the brownies in the baking dish before the icing starts to harden. Let cool completely. When the icing is set, cut the brownies into 1 to 2-inch squares you can pop in your mouth.

## Deer Angie's Brownie Icing

- ¼ cup unsweetened cocoa powder
- ¼ cup (½ stick) butter, at room temperature
- ¼ cup whole milk
- 1 cup granulated sugar
- 1 teaspoon vanilla extract

Place the cocoa powder, butter, milk, and sugar in a saucepan over medium heat. Bring to a rolling boil, stirring constantly. Boil for 2 to 3 minutes, until the sugar is completely dissolved. Remove from the heat and stir in the vanilla. Blend with a handheld electric mixer on low speed (or by hand) for 1 minute.

Skim the top of the mixture with a spoon to remove any floating cocoa powder. Let cool briefly, until the icing is of spreadable consistency.

*notes* _____

_____

_____

_____

_____

_____

## SUGAR MOMMAS TIPS

*carpool crunch:* Forego the double boiler—place the butter and chocolate in a glass or other microwave-safe bowl and heat on high power in 30-second intervals, stirring in between, until melted.

*sass it up:* Use Valrhona unsweetened cocoa powder. For an extra-indulgent experience, use whipping cream in lieu of milk.

If you want to get fancy, put the brownie squares in decorative baking cups to serve at a party.

# Peach Queen Cobbler

*Submitted by Brooke Schumann Halverson and Rex Ann Schumann Hill*
*From their grandmother Esther Schumann's recipe, Albert, Texas*

As children, Brooke and Rex Ann spent June through September collecting peaches from the family ranch nestled in Texas Hill Country. The peaches were so bountiful that the sisters would grab a bushel and take them over to Grandmother Esther's house and start cooking. They would make peach pie, peach preserves, and peach cobbler. Once their peaches were peeled, sliced, and baked, the girls would celebrate the season by heading over to the Stonewall Peach JAMboree and Rodeo.

Esther and her husband, Otto, took pride in the festivities. The Schumann family settled 5,000 acres of land in Gillespie County, Texas, just outside of Fredericksburg, in 1867. They grew several varieties of peaches on their ranch, including Springgold, Red Baron, and Parade, which matured throughout the summer.

Otto Schumann was director of the rodeo at the Peach JAMboree for more than 40 years. Brooke and Rex Ann remember their granddaddy building the arena. The rodeo was a community affair, and the entire extended family got involved. Aunt Karen was runner-up for Peach Queen, and her sister-in-law, Carolyn, was an actual Peach Queen! Sisters Brooke and Rex Ann didn't need the thrill of a competition, when their activities and this cobbler kept them entertained all summer along. We award this creation a blue ribbon!

{ *The family's peaches were enjoyed in the White House kitchen during the Johnson administration.*

# Peach Queen Cobbler SERVES 6 TO 8

1   cup granulated sugar

1   cup all-purpose flour

1   tablespoon baking powder

1/8   teaspoon salt

3/4   cup whole milk

1/2   teaspoon vanilla extract

1/2   cup (1 stick) unsalted butter

2   cups peaches, peeled, pitted, and sliced 1/3 inch thick

1/2   cup packed dark brown sugar

2   teaspoons ground cinnamon

Calf scramble

Preheat the oven to 350°F. Place the granulated sugar, flour, baking powder, and salt in a large bowl and whisk together. Stir in the milk and vanilla, mixing until a smooth batter forms.

To assemble the cobbler, place the butter on the bottom of a 9-inch square baking dish. Place the dish in the oven for about 2 minutes, until the butter is melted and the baking dish is warmed. Remove the dish from the oven and pour the batter on top of the butter. Do not stir them together. Place the peaches on top of the batter in a decorative pattern. Using your hand, sprinkle the brown sugar evenly over the peaches. Sprinkle the cinnamon evenly over the top. Bake for 55 to 60 minutes, until the crust is golden. Remove from the oven and let cool for 15 to 20 minutes before serving. Serve alone or with vanilla ice cream.

notes

_____

_____

_____

_____

_____

_____

_____

_____

_____

_____

_____

*sugar mommas note:* During the baking process, the butter and batter undergo some cosmic scientific transformation, causing them to mingle, turn golden, and caramelize. Each bite propels you straight to sugar heaven.

*modern variation:* Try this cobbler with blackberries, blueberries, strawberries, or mangoes.

# Apple Crisp

*Submitted by Mark Sommer*
*From his grandmother Helen Lee's recipe, Louisville, Kentucky*

At the young age of 106, Helen Lee has lived a very full life. Born in Kentucky, she lived in New Orleans during the time of segregation imposed by Jim Crow laws, and then in Chicago at the start of the Depression. In 1940, Helen persuaded the family to move to Los Angeles in search of a warmer climate.

Helen was a concert pianist, and music must be her fountain of youth. Her grandson, Mark, told us, "To put her age in perspective, her first job was playing an organ at a theater featuring silent movies." She did not marry until roughly 30, which was just short of ancient in those days. Helen's husband loved to entertain, and Mark believes that may explain why his grandmother was such a great cook. By the time Mark was old enough to partake in their frequent dinner parties, each meal was a major culinary experience. Whether it was a scrambled-egg breakfast or a four-course dinner, nobody could match Helen's cooking skills.

For this apple crisp, Helen's advice is: "You can never use too much butter." We think that applies to most delicious things in life.

{ *Helen's advice is: "You can never use too much butter" We think that applies to most delicious things in life.*

# Apple Crisp SERVES 6 TO 8

2 cups packed light brown sugar

2 cups all-purpose flour

10 tablespoons (1¼ sticks) butter, at room temperature

½ teaspoon vanilla extract

5 Pippin or Granny Smith apples, cored, peeled, and sliced ¼ to ½ inch thick

2 teaspoons fresh lemon juice

½ teaspoon ground cinnamon

Für Elise

Preheat the oven to 375°F. Grease a 12 by 8-inch baking dish (or use nonstick cooking spray) and set aside.

Place the sugar, flour, butter, and vanilla in a large bowl and mix by hand until the topping is well combined, but still crumbly. Place the apple slices on the bottom of the baking dish. Sprinkle the lemon juice over the apples. Spread the topping evenly over the apples. Sprinkle the cinnamon evenly over the top. Bake for 40 minutes, or until the topping is golden brown. Remove from the oven and let cool for 15 minutes before serving. Serve alone or with ice cream.

_notes_ _____

_____

_____

_____

_____

_____

_____

_____

*sugar mommas note:* Because you make the topping by hand, this is a great recipe for kids. All that grit involved with making the crumb topping is like playing with dirt. If you have an aversion to getting muck under your nails, rubber gloves are the answer.

*sass it up:* Snag some vanilla or dulce de leche ice cream to enjoy with your crisp. We love when the warm gooeyness and cold ice cream collide.

# Cherry Slices

*Submitted by Elisa Kletecka Allan*
*From her grandmother Marie Eleanor Vorel Kletecka's recipe, Rockford, Illinois*

"This recipe is from my dad, who got it from his mom . . . whose cake stand I covet and wedding band I cherish."

Elisa vividly remembers her grandmother Marie, a butcher's daughter, from the south side of Chicago. Marie's parents crossed the Atlantic by boat from Czechoslovakia (Bohemia) and settled in Illinois at the time of the Chicago World's Fair in 1893. Marie grew up living above the family butcher shop, where she also raised her son and daughter.

{ *Marie was a stoic life force—the glue that held the family together during a tumultuous time.*

When Elisa was 10 years old, her parents divorced. The following year, Elisa and her father, Edward, went to live with his mother, who provided a stable and loving environment. Marie was a stoic life force—the glue that held the family together during a tumultuous time. Marie passed away when Elisa was 13. In the hospital, her tiny engraved platinum wedding band, dated June 24, 1933, was cut away from her finger. Elisa's dad presented her with the ring, advising her to have it repaired. Refusing to alter it, Elisa wears the heirloom (still severed) on her ring finger daily, with the cut on the palm side of her hand. She is very mindful of it so it doesn't catch on anything. It serves as a constant memento of her grandmother.

Before Elisa married, she began collecting cake stands. She became aware of a white milk glass cake stand her father had inherited from Marie, with the edges trimmed in kelly green. She had never seen anything like it before. She asked her father, Edward, if she could have it, and he said yes, but . . . not yet.

At Elisa's request, Edward served these Cherry Slices at her wedding shower in honor of Marie.

# Cherry Slices MAKES ABOUT 2 DOZEN 2-INCH SQUARE BARS

3 cups all-purpose flour

1½ teaspoons baking powder

1 teaspoon salt

1 cup (2 sticks) butter, at room temperature

1¾ cups granulated sugar

½ cup packed light brown sugar

4 large eggs

1 teaspoon vanilla extract

1 (21-ounce) can cherry pie filling

¼ cup confectioners' sugar, for dusting

A treasured heirloom

Preheat the oven to 350°F. Grease an 11 by 17-inch rimmed baking sheet (or use nonstick cooking spray). Set aside.

In a large bowl, whisk together the flour, baking powder, and salt. Set aside. Place the butter and both sugars in the bowl of a stand mixer fitted with the paddle attachment and beat on medium speed until creamy. Add the eggs, one at a time, and mix on low speed until well blended. Add the vanilla. Add the flour mixture, a little at a time, and beat until smooth. Reserve 1 cup of the batter.

Spread the remaining batter in the baking sheet. Spoon the cherry filling over the top. Drop the reserved cup of batter by teaspoonfuls over the pie filling. It should look uneven. When baked, the batter on the bottom rises and creates reservoirs of cherry filling.

Bake for 30 to 35 minutes, until the batter begins to turn golden. Remove from the oven and let cool completely. Dust with confectioners' sugar. Cut into 2-inch squares.

○ ○ ○
○       ○
○ *notes* ○ _____
○       ○
○ ○ ○

_____

_____

_____

_____

_____

_____

_____

_____

_____

_____

_____

_____

_____

_____

_____

_____

_____

_____

_____

_____

_____

*sass it up:* Go gourmet—we recommend Clearbrook Farms Cherry Tart Filling or Chukar Sour Cherry Pie and Cobbler Filling.

*modern variation:* Get creative and try your favorite pie filling: apricot, blueberry, apple cinnamon, or apple raisin.

# Blueberry Buckle

*Submitted by Nancy Dougherty Spears*
*From her mother Dolly Mae Taylor Dougherty's recipe, Ocala, Florida*

Dolly Mae Taylor was born in Cincinnati in 1920, but she grew up and went to college in New Orleans. She was an adventurous woman for the era, the first to graduate from Louisiana State University with a degree in commercial aviation. After an unsuccessful first marriage, she found true love in handsome Air Force pilot Raymond E. "Doc" Dougherty. Like most women of that time, Dolly dropped her career aspirations and devoted her life to supporting her family's needs—in this case, the nomadic path of a "serviceman."

As a homemaker, Dolly approached cooking with the same bravado as aviation. She dove right in! Thus, Dolly's cooking was inspired by her varied surroundings—the German and English immigrants who settled Cincinnati, spiced by the Cajun and Creole influences of New Orleans. She studied the foods of Hawaii when the family lived there in the early 1950s and Chinese and Japanese cooking while they were stationed in Japan. They eventually settled in Ocala, Florida, when their youngest daughter, Nancy, was still a child.

When Nancy was eight or nine, Dolly went to work at the public library (she was the children's librarian widely known in Ocala as Miss Dolly), and Doc took over the domestic duties of cooking and cleaning. Dessert was not Doc's forte, but Nancy enjoyed baking whenever possible. Doc didn't particularly care for Nancy making a big mess in his kitchen with her cake batter escapades.

Nancy moved to Orlando to go to college at 19 and remained there working for Lockheed Martin after she graduated. Dolly and Doc would come to Orlando once a month to visit Nancy and shop at the Navy exchange. After shopping, they would meet their daughter for lunch, and Dolly would always bring a dessert that Nancy could take back to the office and share with co-workers. Dolly's visits were a popular day at work, and everyone knew Nancy's mom through her baked goods. Nancy is certain Dolly's baking contributed to her job security. It must have worked, since Nancy has been with the company for over 25 years.

Blueberry Buckle was a favorite treat in Dolly's repertoire. Though the family migrated regularly, Dolly's sweets were a constant, providing Nancy with a sense of home wherever they happened to land.

# Blueberry Buckle MAKES 16 (2-INCH) SQUARES

## TOPPING

½  cup granulated sugar

⅓  cup all-purpose flour

½  teaspoon ground cinnamon

¼  cup (½ stick) butter, at room temperature

## BOTTOM

2  cups all-purpose flour

2  teaspoons baking powder

½  teaspoon salt

¾  cup granulated sugar

¼  cup (½ stick) butter, at room temperature

1  large egg

½  cup whole milk

2  cups fresh or thawed frozen blueberries

USAF pin

Preheat the oven to 375°F. Butter and flour a 9-inch square baking dish (or use nonstick baking spray with flour).

**To prepare the topping:** Place the sugar, flour, cinnamon, and butter in a large bowl. Use your hands to mix them together and set aside. If you recently got a manicure, use a fork instead of your hands.

**To prepare the bottom:** In a medium bowl, whisk together the flour, baking powder, and salt. Set aside. Place the sugar and butter in the bowl of a stand mixer fitted with the paddle attachment and beat on medium speed until creamy. Reduce the speed to low and add the egg. Add half the flour mixture and blend. Slowly incorporate the milk. Add the remaining flour mixture and blend until smooth. Use a wooden spoon or spatula to fold in the blueberries.

Pour the batter into the baking dish and spread it evenly. Sprinkle the topping over the batter. Bake for 45 to 50 minutes, until a toothpick inserted in the center comes out clean. Remove from the oven and let cool completely. The buckle may be eaten for dessert, breakfast, or anytime in between.

notes _____
_____
_____
_____
_____
_____
_____
_____
_____
_____
_____
_____
_____
_____
_____
_____
_____

## SUGAR MOMMAS TIPS

*sass it up:* Try this recipe with raspberries, cherries, blackberries, or mixed berries.

*old school:* Dolly used vegetable shortening in lieu of butter.

TRANSATLANTIC CHOCOLATE
TRUFFLES

SEASIDE TOFFEE

PEANUT BRITTLE

WHOOPIE PIES

MAGIC MARSHMALLOW PUFFS

CHURCH WINDOWS

BOURBON BALLS

RUM BALLS

FLOATING ISLANDS

CHOCOLATE HYDROGEN BOMBS

# candy and creative confections

If you have unfulfilled aspirations of being a scientist, pull out that elementary-school science kit (beakers, goggles, and liquid potions) and get ready to experiment. Unplug the stand mixer. Put the food processor to rest. Move to the stovetop. Break the baking routine. With a candy thermometer and some waxed paper, you can create magic and see the miracle of butter and sugar transform into candy and creative confections.

We have some outrageous recipes on these pages that will make you want to throw a dinner party just to impress your friends: Chocolate Hydrogen Bombs, Bourbon Balls, Magic Marshmallow Puffs, Church Windows, and Floating Islands. If you want to stay mainstream, try Seaside Toffee, Peanut Brittle, or Transatlantic Chocolate Truffles. Whether you choose to proceed with caution or with zeal, do not overlook the Whoopie Pies! Serve up any confection in this chapter—large, mini, rolled, or dipped—and you'll have the entire neighborhood trailing behind you, begging for more.

Ignite your burners and earn major bragging rights. The lucky recipients may start referring to you as candy queen, cooking fool, or just plain genius.

# Transatlantic Chocolate Truffles

*Submitted by Tracy Girdler*
*From her grandmother Esther Mason's recipe, New York, New York*

Esther Mason ("Omi" to her granddaughter, Tracy) grew up in "The City" and studied fashion at the Otis Parsons School of Design in the late 1930s and early 1940s. Her artistic ability extended beyond fashion design and into the kitchen. Omi made extraordinary truffles and shared the recipe with her daughter, Andrea Girdler, who bestowed the dense chocolate morsels on ambassadors around the world.

Andrea's husband, Lewis Girdler, was a United States diplomat. Andrea made these "little treasures" for friends, acquaintances, and colleagues in Washington, DC; Brazil; Spain; Italy; China; Kenya; and Iceland. Friends from overseas asked for the recipe and the truffles were served to dignitaries at American and foreign embassies on most continents around the globe.

During Officer Girdler's diplomatic tour, he and Andrea lived in Rome for 10 years, and Omi's truffles were always in demand. Whenever they went to an event, Andrea was expected to supply them. We can't be too far from world harmony when even international peacekeepers have discovered sugar diplomacy.

{ *We can't be too far from world harmony when even international peacekeepers have discovered sugar diplomacy.*

# Transatlantic Chocolate Truffles MAKES ABOUT 4 DOZEN TRUFFLES

| | | | |
|---|---|---|---|
| 10 | ounces dark chocolate | 2 | tablespoons dark rum |
| 2 | tablespoons water | 2 to 3 | tablespoons unsweetened cocoa powder, for rolling |
| 1 | cup confectioners' sugar | | |
| 1/3 | cup heavy whipping cream | | |

*Frommer's travel guides*

Place the chocolate and water in the top of a double boiler (or in a metal bowl nestled over a saucepan of boiling water) and stir over medium-low heat until the chocolate is melted, about 8 minutes. Pour the chocolate into a large bowl. Add ½ cup of the sugar and half of the cream and blend well. Add the remaining ½ cup sugar and the remaining cream and blend well. Stir in the rum. Using your spoon or a handheld electric mixer on low speed, beat the chocolate mixture until smooth. Cover the mixture with plastic wrap, making sure the wrap is directly touching the chocolate (so a skin does not form), and chill for at least 50 minutes.

Place waxed paper on a work surface and pour the cocoa powder in a mound in the center. Use a small melon ball scoop or a teaspoon to scoop the chilled chocolate mixture. Roll it between the palms of your hands to form a ball. Then roll the ball in the cocoa powder, coating it thoroughly. Repeat with remaining chocolate mixture. Layer the truffles between sheets of waxed paper in an airtight container and refrigerate. Remove them from the refrigerator 30 minutes before serving.

*notes*

*sugar mommas note:* Andrea suggests using Lindt Excellence 70 percent or Trader Joe's Pound Plus 72 percent dark chocolate. "The darker the chocolate the healthier it is. So these little darlings are good for us!" she says.

*sass it up:* Make these truffles with your favorite liqueur instead of the rum. May we suggest Grand Marnier, Frangelico, Campari, or Chambord?

*modern variation:* In lieu of unsweetened cocoa powder, roll your truffles in finely chopped nuts, chocolate sprinkles, confectioners' sugar, or shredded coconut.

# Seaside Toffee

*Submitted by Jill Stuart*
*From her mother Darlene Bowen's recipe, Arcadia, California*

Jill, who lives near the seashore, and her mother, Darlene, have an annual tradition of making Seaside Toffee at Jill's house for the holidays. Every year, the duo channel Lucy and Ethel, making toffee and packaging it in festive decor such as holiday tins, window boxes, or cellophane bags tied with a ribbon. The ladies deliver their candy to teachers, clients, neighbors, friends, and family. They make certain that everyone receives their fair share to ensure that "toffee wars" do not ruin the holiday spirit.

{ *They make certain that everyone receives their fair share to ensure that 'toffee wars' do not ruin the holiday spirit.*

# Seaside Toffee MAKES 3 TO 4 POUNDS TOFFEE

2 cups finely chopped toasted almonds (divided)

24 ounces semisweet chocolate chips (about 4 cups, divided)

2 cups (4 sticks) butter, at room temperature

2 cups granulated sugar

3 tablespoons water

1 tablespoon vanilla extract

Shovel and pail

Spread ½ cup of the toasted almonds (see Sugar Mommas Notes) in a single layer across an ungreased 15½ by 12-inch rimmed baking sheet. Next, spread 2 cups of the chocolate chips evenly across the sheet and set aside until the toffee is prepared.

Melt the butter in a saucepan over medium heat. Stir in the sugar and water. Continue to stir occasionally until the sugar dissolves. Bring the mixture to a soft boil and continue cooking, stirring only occasionally, until the mixture has a peanut butter color and a candy thermometer reads 300°F (about 25 minutes). This is the hard-crack stage, when syrup dropped into ice water will separate into threads that will break immediately when bent. Remove the mixture from the heat and add the vanilla and ½ cup of the remaining almonds. Stir well to combine. Carefully pour the toffee on the baking sheet over the nuts and chocolate. Cool for 5 to 10 minutes, until the candy begins to set. Sprinkle the remaining 2 cups chocolate chips over the toffee. Use a knife or an angled spatula to spread the chocolate evenly over the toffee as it begins to melt. Spread the remaining 1 cup almonds over the chocolate. Place the baking sheet in a cool, dry place to set overnight. Use a knife to break it into pieces. Store in an airtight container.

## SUGAR MOMMAS TIPS

*sugar mommas notes:* Do not attempt to make Seaside Toffee in humid weather, as it will not set up. For the perfect consistency, make this candy in dry, cold weather.

To chop almonds, place them in a food processor and pulse until the nuts are the desired size.

To toast almonds, place them in a single layer on a baking sheet lined with parchment paper. Bake at 350°F for 5 to 10 minutes, until the nuts are slightly browned.

*modern variation:* Make English Toffee Topping for everyone on your holiday list. After breaking the toffee into pieces, keep the leftover bits—they're a perfect ice-cream topping—and store them in a glass jar covered in holiday fabric. Tie with a decorative ribbon, attach a 3 by 5 handmade card, and voilà!

Visit www.SugarSugarRecipes.com for a video demonstration.

# Peanut Brittle

*Submitted by Jody Potteiger Crabtree*
*From her mother Sherry Tyson Potteiger's recipe, Collegeville, Pennsylvania*

In the 1950s, Sherry Tyson and her siblings milked the family cow each morning on their small farm in Pennsylvania. They strained the milk through cheesecloth into a gallon jar. The cream would rise to the top, and their mother, Kathryn, would ladle it off. The kids then churned it into butter when they had accumulated enough cream, once or twice a week. Churning the butter was quite a chore because it was labor intensive and took *forever*.

During the holidays, the Tyson family traveled to Souderton, Pennsylvania, to acquire peanuts from the local distributor, Landis. They used the peanuts, along with the butter they had churned, to make this brittle as a holiday gift.

{ *Churning the butter was quite a chore because it was labor intensive and took forever.*

# Peanut Brittle MAKES ABOUT 2½ POUNDS BRITTLE

Note: This recipe requires a candy thermometer.

- 2 cups granulated sugar
- 1 cup light corn syrup
- ½ cup water
- 1 cup (2 sticks) butter, cut into slices, at room temperature

- 2 to 3 cups unsalted unroasted shelled peanuts
- 1 teaspoon baking soda

Dairy cow

Butter two 15½ by 12-inch rimmed baking sheets (do not substitute nonstick cooking spray) and set aside.

Place the sugar, corn syrup, and water in a large saucepan over medium to medium-high heat. Stir to combine and cook until the sugar dissolves. Bring the mixture to a boil and stir in the butter. Continue cooking, stirring only occasionally, until the mixture reaches 230°F on a candy thermometer (about 20 minutes). As the temperature increases, stir regularly so the sugar mixture does not burn.

When the mixture reaches 280°F on a candy thermometer (the soft-crack stage, when the bubbles on top become smaller, thicker, and closer together and when syrup dropped into ice water separates into threads that will bend slightly before breaking), stir in the peanuts. Start with 2 cups and add more according to your taste. Continue stirring constantly until the mixture reaches 305°F (the hard-crack stage, when syrup dropped into ice water separates into threads that will break immediately when bent). Remove from the heat and stir in the baking soda, mixing well. The mixture will become light and foamy.

Carefully pour the mixture evenly onto the two baking sheets. It will be very hot. After about 3 minutes, use a spatula coated in nonstick cooking spray to loosen the brittle from the baking sheets and transfer it to parchment paper. Cool for 5 to 7 minutes longer, then use a knife to break it into pieces. Store in an airtight container.

*notes*

---

---

---

---

---

---

---

---

---

---

---

---

---

---

---

---

---

---

---

---

## SUGAR MOMMAS TIP

*sass it up:* Stir in 1 teaspoon of vanilla after you remove the mixture from the heat, before adding the baking soda. After pouring the mixture onto the baking sheets, dust with sea salt to get that sweet-salty fix. We recommend finely ground French sea salt, available at gourmet food stores.

# Whoopie Pies

*Submitted by Jody Potteiger Crabtree*
*From her grandmother Kathryn Tyson's recipe, Collegeville, Pennsylvania*

It's called a Whoopie Pie, but it's shaped like a cookie and tastes like cake. What the heck is it? We don't need to resolve the controversy—we just know they taste fantastic!

Jody received this recipe from her grandmother Kathryn, who subscribes to the Brethren of Christ Church faith, a religion that dates back to the late 1700s in Pennsylvania. In the early 1940s, a traveling minister stayed with Kathryn's family, bestowing this recipe upon them and tracing its origins through oral history. The minister explained that when someone had leftover cake batter, she would drop rounds onto a baking sheet and bake them like cookies. Once cooled, cream filling was sandwiched between two cookies.

Grandmother Kathryn made whoopie pies for Jody, explaining that when kids saw the surprises in their lunch boxes they would scream, "Whoopie!" Over the years, these treats became so popular that they were elevated from "leftover" to *main attraction*. That's a preacher who left a little slice of heaven in his wake.

{ *Grandmother Kathyrn made whoopie pies for Jody, explaining that when kids saw the surprises in their lunch boxes, they would scream, "Whoopie!"*

# Whoopie Pies MAKES 2 TO 3 DOZEN WHOOPIE PIES

4½ cups all-purpose flour

1 cup unsweetened cocoa powder

1 teaspoon baking powder

½ teaspoon salt

1 cup buttermilk

2 teaspoons baking soda

1 cup (2 sticks) butter, at room temperature

2 cups granulated sugar

2 large eggs

2 egg yolks (whites reserved for filling)

1 cup hot water

1 batch Whoopie Pie Filling (recipe follows)

Lunch box

Preheat the oven to 450°F. Grease baking sheets (or use nonstick cooking spray). Place the flour, cocoa powder, baking powder, and salt in a large bowl. Whisk together and set aside. In a medium bowl, whisk together the buttermilk and baking soda until the lumps are dissolved. Set aside.

Place the butter and sugar in the bowl of a stand mixer fitted with the paddle attachment and beat on medium speed until creamy. Reduce the speed to low, add the 2 whole eggs plus the 2 egg yolks, and beat on medium-low speed until well combined, about 1 minute. Add half of the flour mixture and blend on low speed. Slowly incorporate the buttermilk mixture. Add the remaining flour mixture and blend until combined. Add the hot water and mix until smooth.

Drop heaping teaspoonfuls of the dough onto the baking sheet, leaving at least 2 inches between cookies. Bake for 7 to 10 minutes, until the cookies are set and spring back lightly when touched. Remove from the oven and cool for 1 minute. Transfer from the sheet to a wire rack to let cool completely.

Place a cookie on a work surface, flat side up. Top the cookie liberally with filling. Place a second cookie on top, flat side down, making a little sandwich. Serve immediately, or wrap in plastic to store for up to 3 days at room temperature.

## Whoopie Pie Filling

- **4** cups confectioners' sugar
- **1½** cups vegetable shortening
- **2** egg whites (reserved from the cookies)
- **2** teaspoons vanilla extract
- **¼** cup all-purpose flour
- **¼** cup whole milk

Place the sugar and shortening in the bowl of a stand mixer fitted with the paddle attachment and beat on medium speed until light and fluffy. Reduce the speed to low and blend in the egg whites and vanilla. Add the flour and milk and blend until smooth, about 1 minute.

*notes* _____

_____

_____

_____

_____

_____

## SUGAR MOMMAS TIPS

*sass it up:* Squeeze the pie together, making sure the filling is showing between the cookies. Roll the exposed filling in chocolate sprinkles or mini chocolate chips for a crunch.

*old school:* Kathryn used margarine instead of butter.

Sour milk was used in lieu of buttermilk. To make sour milk, measure 1 tablespoon of vinegar into a 1-cup measuring cup, then fill it to the top with milk.

# Magic Marshmallow Puffs

*Submitted by Kevin Listen*
*From his mother Janet Sue Holland Listen's recipe, Groom, Texas*

Janet Sue Holland grew up in Groom, Texas, a town of eight square miles with one stoplight. She married and moved to the significantly larger municipality of Greeley, Colorado. In the 1960s, Janet came across a recipe for Magic Marshmallow Puffs and created her own version to serve to her two very active sons, Kevin and Kregg.

When not in school, the Listen family headed northwest to their ranch along the Laramie River. November through May, the country road was blanketed by snow, and there was no access to the ranch except by snowmobile. The boys frolicked in the snow every day, all day long. Sopping wet and starving, they'd come home at sundown to one of their favorite suppers of big shrimp hero sandwiches, chipped beef on toast, or chili, followed by Magic Marshmallow Puffs. Kevin says the meal may have been light on fruits and vegetables, but it was considered their "dream dinner."

> *Sopping wet and starving, they'd come home at sundown to one of their favorite suppers of big shrimp hero sandwiches, chipped beef on toast, or chili, followed by Magic Marshmallow Puffs.*

Kevin never grew tired of the mystery of the marshmallow puffs. Once baked, the marshmallow simply evaporated. He's still wondering, "Where'd it go?" One was left with a warm puffed pastry with delicious cinnamon-sugar goo inside. Now Kevin makes this treat for his four children on lazy weekend mornings.

Kevin hesitated before submitting this recipe because he thought it was not fancy enough for our "highbrow" cookbook. *What?* Oh, you are so wrong, Mr. Listen! Magic Marshmallow Puffs are a fabulous recipe created by a mom to serve to her babes after a long, cold day snowed in at the ranch. If it makes our eyebrows pop up, it's highbrow enough for us! This recipe embodies the *Sugar, Sugar* spirit.

# Magic Marshmallow Puffs MAKES 24 PUFFS

¼ cup (½ stick) butter, melted

½ cup cinnamon sugar (see Old School tip)

3 packages (8 pieces each) Pillsbury Original Crescent Rolls

24 large marshmallows (see Momma Reiner's Homemade Marshmallows, page 269)

1 batch Magic Marshmallow Puff Icing (recipe follows)

Rabbit in a hat

Preheat the oven to 375°F. Liberally butter two standard 12-cup muffin pans (or use nonstick cooking spray). Place the melted butter in a small bowl. Place the cinnamon sugar in another small bowl.

On a lightly floured work surface, remove the crescent dough from the packaging and carefully unroll each flat triangular section as you go (no need to separate in advance). Dip 1 marshmallow in the melted butter, then roll it in the cinnamon sugar. Wrap the marshmallow tightly in one triangle of dough, rolling from the wide end and tucking under the edges until the marshmallow is completely sealed in dough. Place it in one cup of the muffin pan. Repeat with the remaining marshmallows and dough. Bake for 10 to 12 minutes, until golden brown. Remove from the oven and cool for 1 to 2 minutes. Arrange the warm puffs on a serving plate and drizzle with the icing. Enjoy while warm and fresh from the oven.

## Magic Marshmallow Puff Icing

1   cup confectioners' sugar

1 to 2 tablespoons whole milk

½   teaspoon vanilla extract

Place the confectioners' sugar in a large bowl. Slowly whisk in the milk until the icing reaches the desired consistency—thin enough to drizzle but not runny. Add the vanilla and mix well.

*notes* _____

_____

_____

_____

_____

## SUGAR MOMMAS TIPS

*sugar mommas note:* Do not deny yourself one of life's greatest pleasures. Many of our testers declared this their favorite recipe in the book. We call it the "bad mood buster." If you've had a bad day, broken up with somebody, or gotten depressed by the stock market, make these Magic Marshmallow Puffs and see your frown disappear.

*sugar mommas alert:* The marshmallows disintegrate into warm, delicious goop. Kevin's wife, Amy, claims you are supposed to take a fork to mush the goop around the roll so that every bite is drenched in cinnamon-sugar butter. We just popped the rolls from the pan into our mouths, never stopping for plates or forks!

*old school:* If you don't have premixed cinnamon sugar lying around, make your own by mixing ½ cup granulated sugar with 1 tablespoon ground cinnamon.

# Church Windows

*Submitted by Lori Bendetti*
*From her grandmother Malissa Elizabeth Claxton Starnes's recipe, Waco, Texas*

Lori Bendetti looked forward to Mamaw (Malissa Starnes) and Papaw's (Ellison Trine Starnes Sr.) visits during Thanksgiving and Christmas, because she knew Mamaw would bring one of her specialties, Church Windows, for dessert. Mamaw was originally from Nashville, Tennessee, and moved to Waco, Texas, when she married Papaw, a Church of Christ minister. As a preacher's wife, Mamaw traveled with her husband as he sermonized throughout the region. Although they were on the road, to maintain the comforts of home, Mamaw was known to wake up at 12:00 A.M. to make Papaw his "midnight snack." *That* is devotion.

Lori says Mamaw was a true Southern belle. Apparently everyone else had the same opinion of Ms. Starnes. In May 1997, then governor George W. Bush commissioned her a "Yellow Rose of Texas." This award, given only through the Office of the Governor, recognizes outstanding Texan women for their "significant contributions to their communities and to Texas in the preservation of our history, the accomplishments of our present, and the building of our future."

Being proper Texans, the holiday get-togethers were scheduled around television coverage of the Dallas Cowboys. While the family was engrossed in the football game, Lori would sneak a few Church Windows slices as an "appetizer" from the silver-footed dish on the buffet table. The vintage pastel-colored treats are irresistible!

> *In May 1997, then governor George W. Bush commissioned her a "Yellow Rose of Texas."*

# Church Windows MAKES ABOUT 3 DOZEN 1-INCH SLICES

1  (10.5-ounce) package pastel-colored mini marshmallows

½  cup finely chopped pecans (optional)

½  cup (1 stick) butter, at room temperature

6  ounces semisweet chocolate

1  large egg, beaten

1  cup confectioners' sugar

Dallas Cowboy cheerleaders

Place the marshmallows, and nuts, if desired, in a large bowl and set aside. Melt the butter and chocolate in a small saucepan over medium-low heat, stirring often, until smooth. Remove the saucepan from the heat and let cool for 20 minutes.

While the mixture is cooling, lay out three 12-inch-long sheets of aluminum foil on a work surface. Place parchment paper on top of each sheet of foil.

When the chocolate mixture has cooled, stir in the egg and sugar and mix until a thick paste forms. Pour the mixture over the marshmallows and pecans in the bowl and stir to coat. Spoon about one-third of the mixture lengthwise down the center of one sheet of parchment paper. Roll the mixture, using the parchment to form a log about 12 inches long and about the diameter of a paper-towel roll insert. Fold the ends of the parchment over the log to wrap it, and then fold the foil around it. Repeat with the two remaining segments. Refrigerate overnight. Remove the logs from the refrigerator and use a serrated knife to cut them into 1-inch slices. Serve cold.

notes

## SUGAR MOMMAS TIPS

*sugar mommas note:* To make perfect logs, use a bamboo sushi mat on top of the parchment paper. Use the mat and your hands to form the log until the desired shape is achieved.

*sugar mommas alert:* Consuming raw or undercooked eggs poses a potential health risk, especially to pregnant women, the elderly, young children, and other highly susceptible individuals with compromised immune systems. We all dipped our fingers in the cake and cookie batter as kids and lived to tell about it (we still do); however, please use good judgment.

*old school:* Malissa used margarine in lieu of butter.

# Bourbon Balls

*Submitted by Perry Richards*
*From his great-grandmother-in-law Julia May Payne Cunningham's recipe,*
*Nowata, Oklahoma*

Perry whipped up his first batch of bourbon balls to impress his girlfriend, Kerrie Comeaux, and her family, especially her grandfather, who was a bourbon man. Perry was aware that Kerrie's grandfather William Patrick "Pat" Cunningham was the grandson of a famous and celebrated Cherokee Native American. He also knew that Pat had a love for that "firewater," as he liked to call it, and would appreciate a creative concoction made with his favorite swill. After savoring a few of these treats, Pat was reminded of the balls his mother used to make in the 1940s, after Prohibition ended. Pat's mother was Julia May, daughter of Julius Czar Payne (1870—1940).

Pat was inspired to tell Perry the story of his grandfather Julius, who in 1897 was the first Native American ever to be named United States Deputy Marshall of Vinita, a territory of Oklahoma before it became a state. Thus began a 40-year career in law enforcement that culminated when Julius became the chief of police of Nowata, Oklahoma.

Pat's use of the term *firewater* had come from his grandfather Julius, who explained it was from the origins of grain alcohol. Julius told stories of when beads, jewelry, and food were traded for just a few swigs of the brew. Pat and Perry compared notes, and Pat confided that his mother's balls included the "Dirty Bird," as she liked to call it, which was 101-proof Wild Turkey, the closest thing to firewater she could find.

Pat reminisced that he could only imagine the early versions of bourbon balls in his granddaddy's days. The balls back then presumably would have been made of ground dry corn, sugarcane, and that good old firewater. He said it was too bad his granddaddy didn't bring any bourbon balls as a peace offering to his famed "jungle lunch" with wanted train robbers The Dalton Gang, whom Chief Payne later captured.

Perry is still impressing people with his confections, which are crowd-pleasers and a hit at holiday parties. Today, multiple boxes of these Bourbon Balls are auctioned off at an annual charity bake sale and fetch upward of $125 per dozen!

# Bourbon Balls MAKES ABOUT 3 DOZEN BALLS

1   (12-ounce) box vanilla wafers (we used Nabisco Nilla Wafers)

1/3   cup granulated sugar

2/3   cup finely chopped walnuts

2/3   cup confectioners' sugar, plus more for dusting

1   tablespoon plus 1 teaspoon unsweetened cocoa powder

2/3   cup bourbon

Firewater

In small batches, place the vanilla wafers in the bowl of a food processor (or in a blender) and grind for 45 seconds, or until finely ground. You should have about 6 cups. Place the granulated sugar in a small bowl and set it aside. Place the wafer crumbs, walnuts, confectioners' sugar, cocoa powder, and bourbon in a large bowl. Use a large spoon or your hands to mix them until all of the bourbon is absorbed.

Use a small melon ball scoop or your hands (see Sugar Mommas Note) to scoop the mixture. Roll it between the palms of your hands to form a ball about the diameter of a quarter. Then roll the ball in the granulated sugar, coating it thoroughly. Repeat with the remaining mixture. Layer the balls between pieces of waxed paper in an airtight container and refrigerate overnight. About 30 minutes before serving, remove the bourbon balls from the refrigerator and dust with confectioners' sugar.

## SUGAR MOMMAS TIPS

_sugar mommas note:_ If using your hands, dip them in confectioners' sugar before you dig into the mound to form balls to prevent sticking.

_sass it up:_ Perry suggests making the balls with 101-proof Wild Turkey, Jim Beam, or Jack Daniel's.

_modern variation:_ Package your Bourbon Balls in a festive tin lined with a padded bottom, waxed paper, or food-safe decorative parchment paper (Wilton sells holiday-themed sheets). Gently place the balls on the paper and dust with confectioners' sugar. Repeat layering the balls with paper and dusting with sugar. Apply a festive label, ribbon, or homemade holiday card.

# cannon family *confections*

*Submitted by Philip Cannon*
*From his mother Josephine Emilie Cannon's recipes, New Orleans, Louisiana*

Josephine Cannon was quite the character. Raised in the Mississippi Delta and New Orleans, she distinguished herself early on by being the first (perhaps only) boarding student ever to break out of the Ursuline Convent in New Orleans. Mrs. Cannon loved good food—especially sweets—and she could cook! One of the families' most cherished memories is of Josephine, at age 95, in a home that cared for Alzheimer's patients, eating large raw oysters in spicy red sauce with saltines and drinking ice-cold beer.

Josephine Emilie Cannon is indelibly etched in our minds. She must have been a Sugar Momma who passed on the sugar gene to her son Philip and his daughter Sarah. Now we can channel Josephine's adventurous spirit through her creative confections, Rum Balls and Floating Islands.

{
- Rum Balls
- Floating Islands
- Chocolate Hydrogen Bombs

# Rum Balls MAKES 3 TO 4 DOZEN BALLS

1   (12-ounce) box vanilla wafers (we used Nabisco Nilla Wafers)

1   cup confectioners' sugar, plus ½ cup more for rolling and dusting

1½  cups finely chopped pecans

1½  tablespoons unsweetened cocoa powder

3   tablespoons light corn syrup

2   teaspoons vanilla extract

½   cup plus 1 tablespoon rum (4.5 ounces)

Mardi Gras beads

In small batches, place the vanilla wafers in the bowl of a food processor (or in a blender) and grind for 45 seconds, or until finely ground. Place ½ cup of the confectioners' sugar in a small bowl and set aside.

Place the wafer crumbs, remaining 1 cup confectioners' sugar, the pecans, cocoa powder, corn syrup, vanilla, and rum in a large bowl. Use a large spoon or your hands to mix all the ingredients until all of the rum is absorbed.

Use a small melon ball scoop or a teaspoon to scoop the mixture. Roll it between the palms of your hands to form a ball about the diameter of a quarter. Then roll the ball in the confectioners' sugar, coating it thoroughly. Repeat with the remaining mixture. Layer the balls between waxed paper in an airtight container and refrigerate overnight. About 30 minutes before serving, remove the container from refrigerator and dust the rum balls with the remaining confectioners' sugar.

# Floating Islands SERVES 8

Philip Cannon clearly remembers having these as a child, particularly when staying home from school. One of the benefits of being very sick was that little Philip could con Mother Cannon into making them. He recalls fluffy meringue clumps floating in pale yellow custard that was as runny as a thick cream soup and was sweeter than even most children could stand.

| | | | |
|---|---|---|---|
| 1 | tablespoon all-purpose flour | 1/8 | teaspoon salt |
| 1¼ | cups granulated sugar (divided) | 1½ | teaspoons vanilla extract |
| 4 | large eggs, separated | 2 | teaspoons ground nutmeg |
| 6 | cups (1½ quarts) cold whole milk, divided | | Doctor's note |

**To make the custard sauce:** Whisk together the flour and 1 cup of the sugar in a small bowl and set aside. Place the egg yolks in the bowl of a stand mixer fitted with the paddle attachment and beat on medium speed for 1 minute. Slowly add the flour mixture to the beaten egg yolks and blend until light and creamy, about 2 minutes. Set aside.

Pour 4 cups of the milk into a large saucepan over medium heat. Add the egg yolk mixture, stirring with a wooden spoon to combine. Add the salt. Stir constantly, scraping down the sides of pot, for 20 to 25 minutes, until the mixture coats the back of the wooden spoon. The consistency will be similar to that of a cream soup. Remove from the heat and stir in the vanilla. Set the custard sauce aside to cool.

**To make the meringue islands:** Place the egg whites in the bowl of a stand mixer fitted with the whisk attachment and beat on high speed until they form soft peaks. With the mixer running, slowly add the remaining ¼ cup sugar and beat until stiff, about 1 minute. Be careful not to overwork the eggs, as they will dry out.

In a large saucepan, heat the remaining 2 cups milk over medium-low heat until tiny bubbles form around the edge of the pot. Using two large spoons, scoop and shape some of the egg white mixture into a large oval mound bigger than an egg. Drop the heaping spoonful of egg white into the milk. Repeat with 2 or 3 more mounds (do not crowd them in the saucepan) and cook for about 4 minutes each, flipping the mounds after 2 minutes. Carefully remove the meringue islands and place them on paper towels while you cook the remaining islands. You want 16 islands total.

When ready to serve, divide the custard sauce evenly among eight bowls. Place 2 meringue islands on top of each. Sprinkle nutmeg very lightly over the top and refrigerate. Serve cold.

*sass it up:* Use cinnamon in lieu of nutmeg. Add a sprig of mint on top of the islands for color.

# Chocolate Hydrogen Bombs

*Submitted by Sarah Underwood*
*From her father Philip Cannon's recipe, Houston, Texas*

The Chocolate Hydrogen Bomb came about when Philip Cannon was in his manic chocolate phase of life, looking for the purest sugar high available, and before anyone knew that some chocolate was good for you. He found a recipe for a classic French chocolate dish that was good but did not have the number of textures that he sought, so it fell by the wayside. Far from being an old family recipe, it was the product of Mr. Cannon's desire to have a multitextured, industrial-strength chocolate dessert. When we asked about the recipe, he said, "We try, we taste, we modify, we pass it on . . . what a great tradition!"

Chocolate Hydrogen Bombs should be illegal. This dessert is so decadent that it seems naughty. It must be wrong, but it tastes so right.

{ *We try, we taste, we modify, we pass it on . . . what a great tradition!*

# Chocolate Hydrogen Bombs SERVES 6

¼ cup (½ stick) butter, at room temperature

¼ cup granulated sugar

½ cup whole milk

1 egg yolk

4 ounces unsweetened chocolate

2 tablespoons plus 2 teaspoons honey

½ teaspoon vanilla extract

1 (7.05-ounce) box amaretti cookies (18 to 24 cookies; see Sugar Mommas Note)

2 tablespoons brandy

1 batch Chocolate Hydrogen Bomb Whipped Cream (recipe follows)

*Elizabeth David's French Country Cooking, 1951*

Place the butter and sugar in the bowl of a stand mixer fitted with the paddle attachment and beat on medium speed until creamy.

In a small saucepan, scald the milk (heating it to just under boiling, when small bubbles form around the edge of the saucepan). Remove from the heat and let cool for 15 minutes. Place the egg yolk in a separate bowl and whisk until smooth. Gradually blend the milk into the yolk and beat well. Set aside.

In a large saucepan, melt the chocolate and honey over low heat, stirring constantly. When the chocolate is melted, slowly add the yolk-milk mixture and mix until well incorporated. Add the creamed butter, one-fourth at a time, making sure to blend well before adding more. Continue to stir the mixture over low heat until the chocolate sauce is smooth. Remove from the heat and stir in the vanilla. Set aside to let cool while you prepare the macaroons.

Place 3 or 4 amaretti in each of six martini glasses or small serving dishes. Drizzle ¼ teaspoon of the brandy over each cookie. Allow them to soak for a couple of minutes. Pour the chocolate sauce over and around the cookies in each dish, allowing the sauce to pool in the bottom. Cover the glasses with plastic wrap and chill for 8 hours or overnight. Bring them to room temperature for 30 minutes before serving. Top with a large dollop of the whipped cream.

## Chocolate Hydrogen Bomb Whipped Cream

1½  cups heavy whipping cream

2  tablespoons granulated sugar

Place the cream in the bowl of a stand mixer fitted with the whisk attachment and beat on high speed until it begins to stiffen, about 90 seconds. Add the sugar and beat until soft peaks form, about 20 seconds longer.

*notes*

*sugar mommas note:* For amaretti cookies, we suggest the following brands, available at Italian specialty stores or online: Balocco, Bonomi, or Lazzaroni.

*modern variation:* In lieu of brandy, use your favorite liquor, such as rum, cognac, or whiskey, or forget the alcohol altogether.

*old school:* Mr. Cannon makes a large bowl of Chocolate Hydrogen Bomb "soup" rather than individual servings. Drizzle ¼ teaspoon brandy over each amaretti. Place a layer of amaretti on the bottom of a large glass soufflé dish (1½ quarts) or crystal bowl. Pour a layer of chocolate sauce over and around these. Add a second layer of amaretti and repeat. Continue to add layers and chocolate until all of the amaretti have been used. Cover tightly with plastic wrap and refrigerate overnight. Bring to room temperature before serving. Top with Chocolate Hydrogen Bomb Whipped Cream and serve.

*carpool crunch:* Use store-bought whipped topping.

# Chocolate Hydrogen Bomb Cocktail (aka Booze Shake) SERVES 4

As an alternative to the Chocolate Hydrogen Bomb, Mr. Cannon whips out this "grown-up dessert" on the spur of the moment. A modified version of the Velvet Hammer cocktail, it is fast, easy, and tasty—the usual result of combining things that are very good on their own.

1 cup vanilla or coffee ice cream, softened

2 tablespoons (1 ounce) liqueur (Tia Maria, Grand Marnier, Kahlúa, amaretto, or crème de cacao)

¼ cup (2 ounces) brandy

¼ cup whole milk (as needed)

2 amaretti cookies, finely crushed

Unsweetened cocoa powder, for dusting (optional)

Place the ice cream, liqueur, and brandy in a blender and mix until smooth. Add milk as needed to achieve a thick but (barely) pourable liquid. Divide evenly among four cocktail glasses. Dust the tops with crushed cookies and cocoa powder and serve.

*notes* _____

_____

_____

_____

_____

_____

_____

_____

_____

## SUGAR MOMMAS TIP

*sass it up:* For festive serving glasses, place a wet paper towel on the counter next to the bowl of crushed cookies. Press the rim of each glass onto the towel to moisten it lightly, then dip the rim into the bowl of cookie crumbs.

CHAPTER

7

recipe
legacies

*"When I walk into my kitchen today, I am not alone. Whether we know it or not, none of us is. We bring fathers and mothers and kitchen tables, and every meal we have ever eaten. Food is never just food. It's also a way of getting at something else: who we are, who we have been, and who we want to be."*

—MOLLY WIZENBERG, FROM *A HOMEMADE LIFE*

*We believe every recipe has a story. It does not matter who you are or where you are from. Recipes evoke memories of adventures, shared holidays and celebrations, life's grand times, and even some low points. Who hasn't face-planted into a piece of pie or an entire pan of brownies after a bad day or a breakup?*

*The best part of looking backward is the secrets these recipes reveal. It's not just mixing a list of ingredients, it is reminiscing as you stir. No birthday really feels complete without a cake and a candle. We sought to discover what makes that cake so special. Here's a clue: It's not about the cake.*

*What do you have lurking in your recipe box? Take a minute to finger through those old index cards and see who or what jumps out. We are sure you will be surprised. You may feel reconnected to your past, like the feeling you get flipping through old photo albums. We assume nobody in the house will object to testing the fruits of your labor.*

*We are grateful for the opportunity to meet so many new friends. Our contributors inspired us inside the kitchen and out. We thought we'd share their insight, so here is what they had to say. Perhaps you will relate to Philip Cannon or connect with Catherine Watson like we did.*

If you give the same recipe to five different people, you will get five dishes as subtly varied and nuanced as the differences among five performances of a piece of classical music. It is the *technique* of the creator that makes the taste come alive and gives us the wonderful variation and textures that we find in life.

There are few pleasures in life more intense than someone we love or admire complimenting us on a sensational dish. The truest testimonial is for that person to ask for the recipe. Beware of anyone who doesn't like dogs or who will not freely share any recipe. Always give away your recipes and ask the recipient how it turned out. At the end of our lives, all we truly have is what we have given away.

**—E. PHILIP CANNON**

Think about it . . . when you're in your twenties, thirties, and forties, and in a group, you like to be referred to as "ladies." Head down the road past 50 and we all smile when we hear "the girls." This particular little group of girls started meeting after about seven of us took an Alaskan cruise together about four years ago. It was a glorious trip where all we did was laugh and eat and shop and eat some more! We all ordered different things, especially at dessert time, when it was always a surprise what we would get. Yet again, fellowship, friends, and *food*!

I've told everybody I want to die with fudge in my teeth! That way I'll know I died smiling. Fudge and Heaven . . . now that's a combo!

**—CATHERINE WATSON**

True foodies get joy and passion from the food they discover and create. It becomes a part of who they are. Because of that, they become people who understand the importance of keeping family recipes that have been handed down alive and honored and moving forward into the future.

**—KATHY GROCOTT**

One reflects the kitchen of his or her childhood. I love to cook, have studied various cuisines, greatly enjoy approaching a new complex recipe from an interesting cookbook, and consider myself at least a gourmand. It's my second-favorite activity, after the guitar, but that's another story. But still, I make the savories at my house and, perhaps because of the division of expertise in my childhood home, have rarely adventured into desserts. Luckily my wife and both daughters love to make them with a passion. And now one of them has even compiled this sweets cookbook (with the other assisting in the test kitchen).

**—JAY DOUGHERTY**

Hard to believe it has been almost 10 years since Mema lovingly assembled her favorite recipes and gave us the original edition of this [family] cookbook. Since that time, the Hudgins family has done a lot of growing, both in terms of size and age. We've added spouses and grandchildren, and spread ourselves out across the country, and some of us have even become adults. We've got our own kids now, and we understand. We no longer just eat—we cook.

And that's what makes this Third Edition special. In addition to Mema's classics, this updated collection contains submissions from each of us and our husbands and wives, recipes that hopefully will become family favorites like those that went before.

Cooking, they say, is a lot like love; it should either be entered into with abandon or not at all.

Here's to abandon!

**—DAVID HUDGINS**

# Momma Reiner's Homemade Marshmallows

*Submitted by Kimberly "Momma" Reiner*

It's never too late to start new rituals and create special family memories. Momma Reiner's Fudge started with an old family recipe, but it was the fudge-dipped marshmallows that garnered the attention of Oprah and Martha Stewart. This delicacy was developed on a whim while stirring fudge one day. I noticed a bag of marshmallows and thought, "I'd bet those would taste good dipped in my fudge." And they did. I then sought to create my own marshmallows suited exactly to my tastes. To inspire you to get creative and courageous in your kitchen, Momma Jenna and I leave you with this final recipe.

> { *It's never too late to start new rituals and create special family memories.*

# Momma Reiner's Homemade Marshmallows MAKES ABOUT 40

Note: You will need a candy thermometer for this recipe.

| | |
|---|---|
| 2 tablespoons plus 1 teaspoon unflavored gelatin | 2 egg whites |
| ½ cup cold water | ½ teaspoon vanilla extract |
| 2 cups granulated sugar | ½ cup cornstarch, plus more for dusting |
| ½ cup light corn syrup | ½ cup confectioners' sugar |
| ½ cup hot water | *Sugar, Sugar* by The Sugar Mommas |
| ¼ teaspoon salt | |

Lightly coat a 12 by 8-inch glass baking dish with nonstick cooking spray. In a small bowl, combine the gelatin and cold water. Set aside to soften while you make the syrup.

Place the granulated sugar, corn syrup, hot water, and salt in a medium saucepan. Cook over medium heat, stirring until the sugar dissolves, about 2 minutes. Continue cooking without stirring until the mixture reaches about 240°F on a candy thermometer (the soft-ball stage, when syrup dropped into ice water may easily be formed into a soft ball with your hands). Remove from the heat. Gently add the gelatin to the syrup mixture, stirring until the gelatin is dissolved. Set the mixture aside.

Place the egg whites in the bowl of a stand mixer fitted with the whisk attachment and beat on high speed until stiff peaks form. Reduce speed to low, and slowly add the syrup mixture. Add the vanilla and continue whipping on high speed for 10 minutes, or until the mixture looks like marshmallow creme.

Use a spatula to pour the mixture into the baking dish and spread evenly. Coat a piece of parchment paper (the size of the dish) with nonstick cooking spray and cover the marshmallow, using your hands to create an even surface. Let the marshmallow set at room temperature overnight before cutting.

Turn the marshmallow out of the baking dish onto a work surface lightly dusted with cornstarch. Lightly coat a sharp knife with nonstick cooking spray and cut the marshmallow into 1½-inch squares. Combine the cornstarch and confectioners' sugar in a bowl. Gently toss the marshmallow squares in the mixture, a few at a time, to coat them lightly. Store at room temperature in an airtight container for up to 1 week.

*notes*

tell us
your story

One of our favorite things to do as Sugar Mommas is to find new, inventive ways to inspire people in the kitchen. If you have a confection, please let us know. The Sugar Mommas want to make it, eat it, and pass it out at carpool. Please deposit your recipe on our Web site, and don't forget to withdraw new ideas while you're there. Or use the form that follows to tell us about traditions you have created in your family. We'd love to hear from you. Happy baking!

—THE SUGAR MOMMAS

www.SugarSugarRecipes.com
e-mail: submit@SugarSugarRecipes.com
fax: 310-454-2604

Follow us online:
Facebook (Sugar, Sugar)—http://www.facebook.com/pages/
Sugar-Sugar/163554640355094

Facebook (Sugar Mommas)—http://www.facebook.com/
pages/The-Sugar-Mommas/302523331303

Twitter (Sugar Mommas)—http://twitter.com/sugarmommas

# Recipe Submission Guide

When you submit a family sweet, we would like to know more than just the edible ingredients. We'd like a glimpse of the family it came from. Please give us some background information. Tell us about where the recipe originated. Share any fun stories and/or things your relative or source are "known for" among family and friends (this could be anything from being a great baker to being addicted to horse races to being able to do a backflip on request—even the most trivial things sometimes make the best tales). How many children/grandchildren did your source have? Was he or she born and raised in a city, or did the person have a rural upbringing? Where did your relative learn how to bake?

Help us paint a portrait using these questions as a guide:

1.  Where did this recipe originate, if you know? Please provide a name, nickname, and city/state. How did your source obtain the recipe?

    _____

    _____

2.  Was it made for a special occasion? Or just whenever the craving arose?

    _____

    _____

3.  Are there any memories that stand out about the recipe? Funny stories?

    _____

    _____

4.  Are there any rituals or traditions related to the recipe?

    _____

    _____

5. What is your favorite memory of the person you associate most with this recipe? Please be specific.

_____

_____

6. Did you or your source change the recipe at all? If so, how and why?

_____

_____

7. Are there any "Modern Variations" to this recipe or ways you like to "Sass It Up?"

_____

_____

8. Are there any "Carpool Crunch" shortcuts you have come across to help speed the time between commencement and enjoyment?

_____

_____

9. What one thing would you most like people to know about the person who gave you this recipe?

_____

_____

# Cake Pan Volumes
# and Tips for Switching Pan Sizes

Many of the cake recipes in this book can be baked in a different size than the pan listed in the instructions. Before switching pans, look at the volume of your batter and determine whether it will appropriately fill another size pan. The chart below lists the capacity of some of the most common cake pans. It is best to fill your pans about half full (unless you're baking very thin layers) and never more than two-thirds full. Deep cake pans should probably only be filled half full to ensure that the middle bakes through.

## *Cake Pan Volume Conversion Chart*

| PAN SIZE | APPROXIMATE VOLUME | |
|---|---|---|
| 1¾ by ¾-inch mini muffin cup | ⅛ cup (2 tablespoons) | |
| 2¾ by 1⅛-inch muffin cup | ¼ cup | |
| 2¾ by 1⅜-inch muffin cup | scant ½ cup | |
| 3 by 1¼-inch large muffin cup | heaping ½ cup | |
| 8 by 1½-inch round cake pan | 4 cups | |
| 8 by 2-inch round cake pan | 6 cups | |
| 8 by 8 by 2-inch square cake pan | 8 cups | |
| 9 by 1½-inch round cake pan | 6 cups | |
| 9 by 2-inch round cake pan | 8 cups | |
| 9 by 9 by 2-inch square cake pan | 10 cups | |
| 13 by 9 by 2-inch rectangular cake pan | 15 cups | |

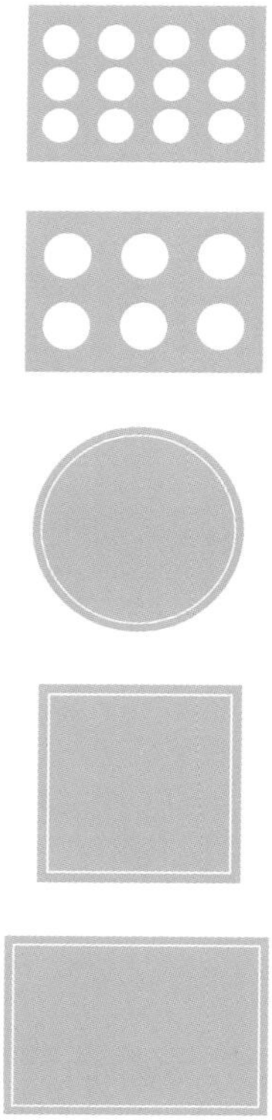

## Tips for Switching Pan Sizes

Baking time varies widely by oven temperature, type of cake batter, and, most important, pan size and depth of batter. If you substitute a similar-size baking pan, such as an 8-inch round for a 9-inch round, you can usually stick to the same general baking time range listed in the original recipe because the depth won't change much.

If you are using a different pan from the one listed in a recipe, try keeping the same oven temperature listed in the recipe but adjusting your baking time up or down according to your pan size. Cupcakes and mini cupcakes take much less time to bake than do other types of cakes—often only 15 to 20 minutes total baking time. Otherwise, in general, the deeper your batter, the longer the baking time. Thus, the larger the pan, the shorter the baking time.

Always watch your cakes carefully, but try to avoid opening the oven door frequently as you will lose 25 to 50 degrees each time it opens. If your cake begins to brown too much at the edges while the center remains liquid, then try reducing your oven temperature. This problem may be a symptom of switching pans, or you may be using a glass baking dish or a dark nonstick pan, which is more prone to causing cakes to brown too quickly around the edges.

Before removing the cake from the oven, check for doneness by inserting a knife or a wooden skewer or toothpick in the center of the cake. If it comes out clean, the cake should be done. And remember to embrace *trial and error*. You can always cover the brown edges with yummy frosting and no one will be the wiser. You'll reach the pinnacle of perfection the next time.

# Metric Conversions and Equivalents

## Metric Conversion Formulas

| TO CONVERT | MULTIPLY |
|---|---|
| Ounces to grams | Ounces by 28.35 |
| Pounds to kilograms | Pounds by .454 |
| Teaspoons to milliliters | Teaspoons by 4.93 |
| Tablespoons to milliliters | Tablespoons by 14.79 |
| Fluid ounces to milliliters | Fluid ounces by 29.57 |
| Cups to milliliters | Cups by 236.59 |
| Cups to liters | Cups by .236 |
| Pints to liters | Pints by .473 |
| Quarts to liters | Quarts by .946 |
| Gallons to liters | Gallons by 3.785 |
| Inches to centimeters | Inches by 2.54 |

## Approximate Metric Equivalents

### WEIGHT

| | |
|---|---|
| ¼ ounce | 7 grams |
| ½ ounce | 14 grams |
| ¾ ounce | 21 grams |
| 1 ounce | 28 grams |
| 1¼ ounces | 35 grams |
| 1½ ounces | 42.5 grams |
| 1⅔ ounces | 45 grams |
| 2 ounces | 57 grams |
| 3 ounces | 85 grams |
| 4 ounces (¼ pound) | 113 grams |
| 5 ounces | 142 grams |
| 6 ounces | 170 grams |
| 7 ounces | 198 grams |
| 8 ounces (½ pound) | 227 grams |
| 16 ounces (1 pound) | 454 grams |
| 35.25 ounces (2.2 pounds) | 1 kilogram |

## LENGTH

| | |
|---|---|
| ⅛ inch | 3 millimeters |
| ¼ inch | 6 millimeters |
| ½ inch | 1¼ centimeters |
| 1 inch | 2½ centimeters |
| 2 inches | 5 centimeters |
| 2½ inches | 6 centimeters |
| 4 inches | 10 centimeters |
| 5 inches | 13 centimeters |
| 6 inches | 15¼ centimeters |
| 12 inches (1 foot) | 30 centimeters |

## VOLUME

| | |
|---|---|
| ¼ teaspoon | 1 milliliter |
| ½ teaspoon | 2.5 milliliters |
| ¾ teaspoon | 4 milliliters |
| 1 teaspoon | 5 milliliters |
| 1¼ teaspoons | 6 milliliters |
| 1½ teaspoons | 7.5 milliliters |
| 1¾ teaspoons | 8.5 milliliters |
| 2 teaspoons | 10 milliliters |
| 1 tablespoon (½ fluid ounce) | 15 milliliters |
| 2 tablespoons (1 fluid ounce) | 30 milliliters |
| ¼ cup | 60 milliliters |
| ⅓ cup | 80 milliliters |
| ½ cup (4 fluid ounces) | 120 milliliters |
| ⅔ cup | 160 milliliters |
| ¾ cup | 180 milliliters |
| 1 cup (8 fluid ounces) | 240 milliliters |
| 1¼ cups | 300 milliliters |
| 1½ cups (12 fluid ounces) | 360 milliliters |
| 1⅔ cups | 400 milliliters |
| 2 cups (1 pint) | 460 milliliters |
| 3 cups | 700 milliliters |
| 4 cups (1 quart) | .95 liter |
| 1 quart plus ¼ cup | 1 liter |
| 4 quarts (1 gallon) | 3.8 liters |

## Oven Temperatures

To convert Fahrenheit to Celsius, subtract 32 from Fahrenheit, multiply the result by 5, then divide by 9.

| DESCRIPTION | FAHRENHEIT | CELSIUS | BRITISH GAS MARK |
| --- | --- | --- | --- |
| Very cool | 200° | 95° | 0 |
| Very cool | 225° | 110° | ¼ |
| Very cool | 250° | 120° | ½ |
| Cool | 275° | 135° | 1 |
| Cool | 300° | 150° | 2 |
| Warm | 325° | 165° | 3 |
| Moderate | 350° | 175° | 4 |
| Moderately hot | 375° | 190° | 5 |
| Fairly hot | 400° | 200° | 6 |
| Hot | 425° | 220° | 7 |
| Very hot | 450° | 230° | 8 |
| Very hot | 475° | 245° | 9 |

## Common Ingredients and Their Approximate Equivalents

1 cup all-purpose flour = 140 grams
1 stick butter (4 ounces • ½ cup • 8 tablespoons) = 110 grams
1 cup butter (8 ounces • 2 sticks • 16 tablespoons) = 220 grams
1 cup brown sugar, firmly packed = 225 grams
1 cup granulated sugar = 200 grams

Information compiled from a variety of sources, including *Recipes into Type* by Joan Whitman and Dolores Simon (Newton, MA: Biscuit Books, 2000); *The New Food Lover's Companion* by Sharon Tyler Herbst (Hauppauge, NY: Barron's, 1995); and *Rosemary Brown's Big Kitchen Instruction Book* (Kansas City, MO: Andrews McMeel, 1998).

indexes

## Geographical Index

# Contributor Index

# Recipe Index